WICKED Kernersville

Wicked Kernersville

ROGUES, ROBBERS, RUFFIANS & RUMRUNNERS

MICHAEL L. MARSHALL
& JERRY L. TAYLOR

The History PRESS

Published by The History Press
Charleston, SC 29403
www.historypress.net

Cover and illustrations by Marshall Hudson

First published 2009

Manufactured in the United States

ISBN 978.1.59629.676.3

Library of Congress Cataloging-in-Publication Data

Marshall, Michael L. (Michael Lee), 1944-
Wicked Kernersville : rogues, robbers, ruffians, and rumrunners / Michael L. Marshall and Jerry L. Taylor.
p. cm.
Includes bibliographical references.
ISBN 978-1-59629-676-3
1. Crime--North Carolina--Kernersville--History--Anecdotes. 2. Violence--North Carolina--Kernersville--History--Anecdotes. 3. Criminals--North Carolina--Kernersville--Biography--Anecdotes. 4. Brigands and robbers--North Carolina--Kernersville--Biography--Anecdotes. 5. Rogues and vagabonds--North Carolina--Kernersville--Biography--Anecdotes. 6. Kernersville (N.C.)--History--Anecdotes. 7. Kernersville (N.C.)--Biography--Anecdotes. 8. Kernersville (N.C.)--Social conditions--Anecdotes. I. Taylor, Jerry L. (Jerry Lee), 1937- II. Title.
HV6795.K47M376 2009
364.109756'67--dc22
2009004894

Notice: The information in this book is true and complete to the best of our knowledge. It is offered without guarantee on the part of the authors or The History Press. The authors and The History Press disclaim all liability in connection with the use of this book.

This book is dedicated to all the men and women who worked at Adams-Millis Plant #4 in Kernersville.

CONTENTS

PREFACE

A little more than three years ago, we began collecting information on the textile mills that, for many years, formed the economic backbone of the town of Kernersville. Eventually, we broadened our search to include all aspects of the town's history.

It was while we were gathering material that we happened across a copy of an article published in 1958 in a newspaper called the *People's News*. Based on an interview with George P. Winfree, who was born in Kernersville in 1885 and lived in the town his entire life, the article was about a man called Banner Jordan, dubbed by Winfree Kernersville's most feared man. In the article, Winfree alleged that in the 1890s, Kernersville was a rough town and the talk of the entire state. In fact, he claimed it was so rough that when the train passed through, the conductor advised passengers to keep a low profile. As Winfree recalled, "This was the day of Banner Jordan, Wick Walker, Ade Walker and others who demanded respect and got it, too."

This account so intrigued us that we decided to look into its claims. As part of our investigation, we had a number of conversations with current and former residents whose families had lived in the town for many generations. From them, we heard several reports that suggested that, indeed, the Kernersville of days gone by was not the sedate place it is today.

Moir Whicker, a well-known and highly respected lifetime citizen of Kernersville, told us that in 1901 his grandfather, a deputy sheriff, was peppered by buckshot when Ade Walker fired a shotgun at him while he was attempting to arrest Walker for drawing a gun and threatening to shoot another man. Phil Thomas McCuiston, whose grandfather operated a bicycle shop in Kernersville in the late 1890s and later a hardware store on North Main Street, related several stories he had heard from his father and grandfather, including some that involved gunplay by local citizens in the vicinity of the hardware store. Jim Winfree supplied us with other thrilling accounts from Kernersville's early days, as well as his own recollections of the old Jordan homeplace, where Banner and his father came to a violent end in 1896 at the hands of revenue agents. Jim also passed along his memory of the Louis Carmichael home mentioned in one of the stories included here.

Armed with tips from these and other Kernersville natives, and with our own research, we headed off to local libraries to examine their reels of microfilm containing images of old newspapers known to cover the area that included Kernersville. With few exceptions, these papers have not yet been indexed, so searching them involved many hours of looking through issue after issue. As old newspaper stories came to light at these and other repositories, it became clear that George P. Winfree knew what he was talking about in the interview he gave in 1958—Kernersville was a pretty rough place in its day. Whether it was a lot rougher than other places of similar size and situation, we can't say, but it was an exciting place for sure.

The stories we gathered also did something else—they opened a window for us onto what life was really like in Kernersville in the late 1800s and early 1900s, when the town was a small, close-knit community and many residents were related or at least knew one another. (You will notice that several of the individuals mentioned in the stories here came from the same family and that some of the families mentioned were closely related to others referenced.)

Eventually, the idea of putting some of the stories into a book emerged, and we directed our effort toward that end. This is our product. We hope you will like reading the stories we have included as much as we enjoyed collecting them. We think they illuminate a side of the town's history not included in other published works. In particular, we believe that, as you read these accounts, you will meet people from the past whose names would otherwise remain unfamiliar to you and learn something of events in Kernersville's history—many tragic—that are rarely, if ever, recalled today.

ACKNOWLEDGEMENTS

We would first like to offer our gratitude to Dr. Eric Hazel for his editorial assistance in reading our manuscript and offering many comments and suggestions for improving it. Because of his help, we believe it is a much better product.

Thanks must also be given to the many fine people at The History Press who helped us through each of the stages of bringing the book to completion: Laura All, commissioning editor, who worked with us from the beginning, answering—cheerfully we might add—all of our questions; Marshall Hudson, senior designer, who provided the illustrations; and Jaime Muehl, project editor.

We would also like to thank the helpful and friendly staffs of the North Carolina Room at the Central Branch of the Forsyth County Public Library in Winston-Salem, the Central Library in Greensboro and the North Carolina Collection of the city of High Point's Public Library. They were always ready to answer our questions or to point out special features of their archival holdings. Thank you very much.

INTRODUCTION

Today, the town of Kernersville, North Carolina, sits at the heart of the Piedmont Triad, surrounded by the nearby cities of Winston-Salem, Greensboro and High Point. It was named after German immigrant Joseph Kerner, who bought land there in 1817. However, it was known in earlier times as Dobson's Cross Roads, a name derived from William Dobson, who began operating a tavern there in 1788. In 1806, Dobson and his son sold their land at the crossroads to Gottlieb Shober, a Moravian living in Salem, who transferred the property to his son Nathaniel, who in turn sold to Kerner.

Following his purchase, Joseph Kerner and his family moved from the Moravian settlement at Friedland, in Forsyth County, and took up residence at the crossroads, where Kerner resided until his death in 1830. His will divided his land among his three children—two sons and a daughter. Son Philip acquired the land containing the tavern, store and post office, which he operated until 1848, when he sold it to William P. Henley.

The period between 1850 and 1860 witnessed the transition of the town, now called Kernersville, from sleepy hamlet to growing village as entrepreneurs from outside began to arrive. The Civil War slowed the town's growth, but it resumed after the war, with tobacco manufacturing becoming a major commercial enterprise. On March 31, 1871, the town was formally incorporated by the North Carolina General Assembly.

In 1873, the railroad came to Kernersville, providing a major economic boost to the economy, and by 1878 its population had increased to some six hundred inhabitants. At that time, it had three tobacco factories and several other businesses besides the usual artisans and mechanics.

Tobacco manufacturing remained the town's major business activity throughout the 1880s but began to wane during the 1890s in the face of competition from big manufacturers such as R.J. Reynolds. As a result,

Kernersville's tobacco factories shifted to the manufacture of textiles around 1900. The town retained its small mill town character for the next seventy years until offshoring of textiles forced it to diversify its economic base.

Today, manufacturing accounts for only one-third of the town's economic activity, a shift that has also spurred growth in its population, which increased by 95 percent between 1990 and 2005. With some twenty-two thousand inhabitants, Kernersville now bears little resemblance to the working-class community that would have been familiar to the individuals described in the following stories.

A BURIED ALIVE SENSATION

Premature Burial

To die is natural; but the living death
Of those who waken into consciousness,
Though for a moment only, ay, or less,
To find a coffin stifling their last breath,
Surpasses every horror underneath
The sun of Heaven, and should surely check
Haste in the living to remove the wreck
Of what was just before, the soul's fair sheath,
How many have been smothered in their shroud!
How many have sustained this awful woe!
Humanity would shudder could we know
How many have cried to God in anguish loud,
Accusing those whose haste a wrong had wrought
Beyond the worst that ever devil thought.

The preceding poem by Percy Russell comes from a 1906 copy of the *Burial Reformer* magazine and aptly illustrates the age-old fear of being "buried alive," a fear that is indeed supported by reports of a substantial number of premature burial stories. In most of these, the burial, or in some cases near-burial, occurs when the individual involved gives an unambiguous appearance of being dead, the condition being introduced as the result of a coma or a similar medical condition.

An interesting case of near-burial appears in the January 11, 1905 edition of the *Greensboro Patriot* under the headline: "Corpse in Coffin Comes to Life." The incident, which took place in Jefferson, Texas, involved an individual named Chidester who was a businessman. According to the story, he "was attacked with a serious illness two days ago and died, according to the attending physician." Following his apparent decease, "an undertaker prepared the body for burial, it was wept over by the family, and on yesterday afternoon, the funeral services were held at the Chidester home. A clergyman delivered a 'powerful' sermon, at the close of which those present were invited to take a last look at the dead." When one of his relatives came forward for a final farewell, she noticed that his lips were moist and cried out that the gentleman in the coffin was alive:

> *A hurried investigation was made and it was discovered that he was breathing. Physicians were quickly summoned and Chidester was removed from the coffin. In a short time he had regained consciousness and was sitting up in bed.*
>
> *He is now able to walk about the house, and if no setback occurs he will be out attending to business in a few days. The coffin was taken back to the undertaker's shop.*
>
> *Chidester has not been told of his narrow escape from being buried alive. It is feared that the shock might be too great for him to bear in his present condition.*

Chidester was one of the lucky individuals, if one believes the statistics compiled by Rodney Davies in a 1998 book called *The Lazarus Syndrome: Buried Alive and Other Horrors of the Undead*. By his estimate, "the percentage of premature burials has been variously estimated as somewhere between 1 per 1,000 to as many as 1 or 2 percent of all total burials in the United States and Europe," a figure he claims increases in times of war or pestilence, when circumstances often necessitate rapid burial.

Many similar incidents are also recounted in a 2001 book by Jan Bondeson titled *Buried Alive: The Terrifying History of Our Most Primal Fear*. One of the more unsettling stories involves an individual who said that during the Great Depression his grandfather had been forced by poverty to "take up a temporary position as a gravedigger in the local churchyard, to aid in the exhumation of coffins for a planned restructuring of the burial ground." It seems he did not last long in the job, confessing to his family "that it had been a horrible experience to see how many of the corpses had been buried alive by mistake." As told in the book, "there were gashed and broken foreheads from pounding the coffin lids, torn fingernails and desperately contorted

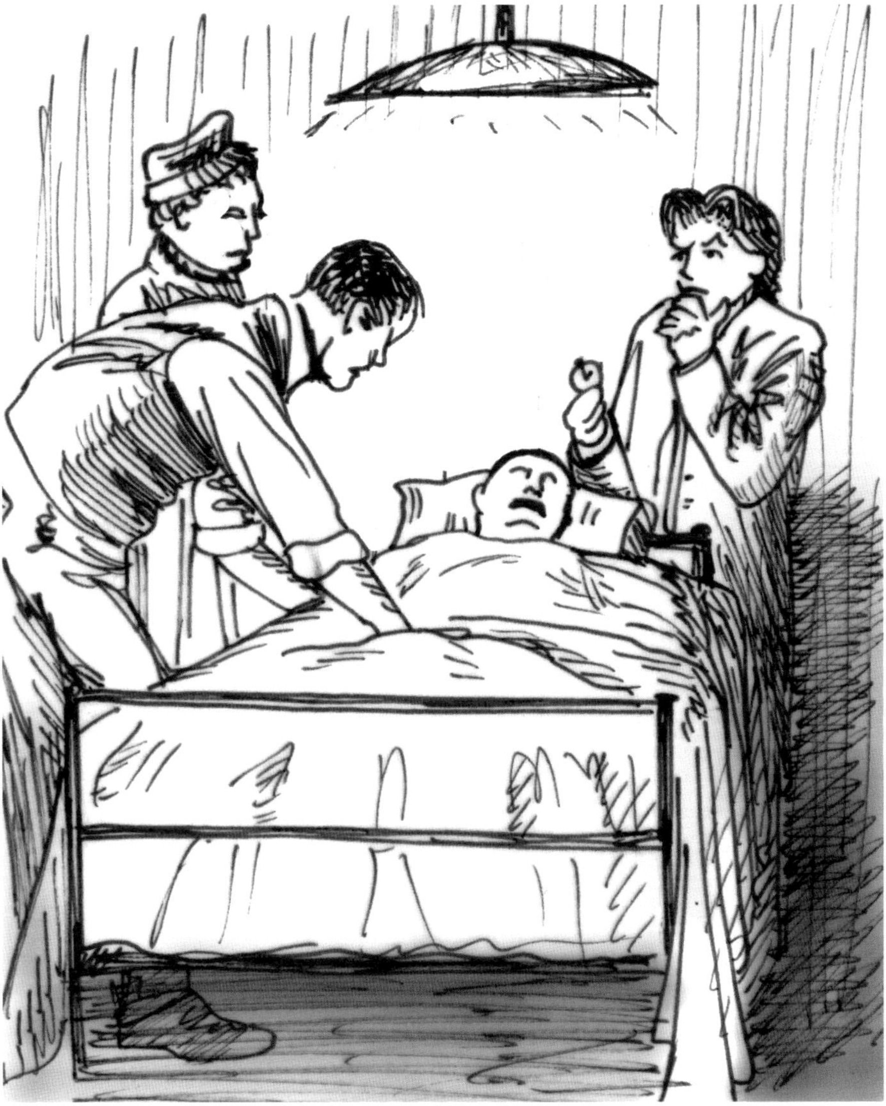

faces that the young gravedigger never forgot." He was especially appalled by the "prematurely buried women who had pulled out their beautiful long hair, which was found wound around their decomposing fingers, or clutched in their skeletal hand[s]."

Bondeson also records a case that came to light just before his book went to print. It appears that on January 25 and 26, 2001, the *Boston Globe* reported the case of a New York woman found lifelessly slumped in her bathtub. Nearby were a suicide note and evidence of a drug overdose.

Upon discovery, police and medical emergency personnel, summoned to the premises, found no signs of life: no pulse, no breathing, turgid skin and unresponsive eyes. The authorities transported her to a nearby funeral home, where the funeral director, who was about to leave, was startled to hear a faint sound of breathing coming from the body bag. When he unzipped it, he discovered that its occupant was alive and quickly had her transported to a hospital, where she recovered.

Pervasive concerns over being buried alive, or burying someone alive, have even triggered a number of inventions intended to allow the "deceased" to signal from the coffin, one of the most recent being a device that received a patent (No. 4,367,461) from the United States Patent Office in 1983.

It seems that the winter of 1884–85 was particularly filled with tales of premature burials. An April 17, 1885 story in the *Landmark* of Statesville, North Carolina, carried the intriguing title "A Buried Alive Sensation." The piece, which the paper had picked up from the *Daily Workman* of Greensboro, reported that "there were never so many sensational stories about persons supposed to have been buried alive as the newspapers have given during the past winter." The paper continued, noting that

> *in some cases these have been downright, unmitigated falsehoods set afloat, representing that certain persons were not dead when interred, and that, upon examination, the supposed dead were found revived out of their trance or stupor and made despairing and horrid exertions to extricate themselves from their dungeon, pulling handfuls of hair from their heads and leaving deep imprints of their finger nails upon the sides and lid of the coffin.*

The paper went on to assert that no matter how "preposterous and false" these stories may have been, they have "had an effect on certain minds." The paper no doubt had in mind a strange incident that had recently taken place in the usually quiet village of Kernersville.

According to an account that first appeared in the April 9, 1885 edition of the *People's Press*, a newspaper published in Salem, North Carolina, a farmer named William Biggs (erroneously called Briggs in some accounts), age fifty-six, was taken ill. Hoping to help cure the poor man, his family transported him to Waughtown, just outside of Salem, where he was placed in a sanitarium operated by Dr. Western G. Hamilton, very likely the same Dr. W.G. Hamilton listed as a physician in Salem in the 1886 edition of *Emerson's Tobacco Belt Directory*.

Biggs was born on March 12, 1829. At age thirty-six he married Mary Standley (a name also seen in some records as Stanley); the marriage took place in Forsyth County on November 17, 1865. Biggs and his wife had several children, including a daughter named Anna.

Unfortunately, Biggs did not recover from his illness, and after "a lingering sickness of two or three weeks," he died at Dr. Hamilton's.

His remains were brought to Kernersville for burial in the Moravian Cemetery. There was no formal funeral, only a graveside service conducted by Reverend C.L. Rights, minister of the local Moravian Church. Reverend Rights, born in 1820, was quite a character in Kernersville and was known to the populace as "Uncle Rights." His wife, Elizabeth Hughes, was also well liked by the citizens and was known as "Aunt Rights."

The trouble started about three hours after Biggs had been interred, when the whispered suggestion began circulating that he had been buried alive. It seems that "great beads of perspiration had been seen on his forehead by several persons." The person who laid out Biggs in the coffin was certain that the man was dead, yet "still those drops of perspiration some were sure they saw was strong witness and could not be set aside."

As might be imagined, there was considerable dithering while the crowd gathered. Finally, town officials were called together and the coroner summoned, and it was decided that disinterment of poor Biggs was the only course of action. The grave was reopened, the coffin pulled out of the ground and the lid removed. After what was certainly a thorough examination, it was determined to everyone's satisfaction that Biggs had indeed not been buried alive, and the body was returned to its final resting place.

Not surprisingly, the Reverend Rights, who had left the cemetery following the service, was shocked when he later returned to find Biggs being exhumed. In fact, Rights was so exercised that he penned an open letter, which was carried in the April 16, 1885 *People's Press*. The good Reverend wrote:

> *I notice the disinterment of William Biggs on the Moravian grave yard here last week, as recorded by the* [Kernersville] News, *has been copied pretty generally. I only kept the burial services at the grave, as the funeral was deferred till some other time. I saw him opened and looked at him for some time, and how anybody could form another idea but what it was in reality, a corpse, never occurred to me, and when a few hours afterwards, I found the grave yard filled with an excited multitude digging out the corpse, I confess it made me feel very strange—for I thought, if he is not dead, I have helped put a great many live people in the ground in the last forty years.*

> *I then first learned that the Town Commissioners had been called together and the disinterment agreed upon. Of course it was all well meant, but I still think that I, in common courtesy, might have been asked my opinion about it.*
>
> *Mr. Biggs is, I believe, the first patient that ever died at Dr. Hamilton's Sanitarium in Waughtown, and I hope the Dr. will not let it happen again.*

Today, a visitor to the Moravian Cemetery will still find Mr. Biggs just where he was finally laid to rest on that exciting day in 1885. The site is marked by several stones now, indicating the graves of William Biggs (March 12, 1829–March 31, 1885), his wife Mary (July 21, 1825–March 11, 1915) and three of their children.

THE LYNCHING OF EUGENE HAIRSTON

Newell Rufus Sapp and his family were well known and highly respected around Kernersville during the nineteenth century. Born in Davidson County, he married Phoebe Farribee, and together they had several children, including Benjamin Jackson, Newell Wesley and Jesse Washington.

Benjamin Jackson became a prominent physician and druggist in Kernersville and also operated the old Sapp Hotel on the town square, which his son, Dr. Carey C. Sapp, later ran as the Kernersville Auto Inn. Benjamin's son Luther L. was also a physician, practicing first in Kernersville and later in Reidsville, North Carolina. Newell Wesley served in the Confederate army and afterward was involved with W.H. Leak and others in Kernersville in the manufacture of plug and twist tobacco, as well as other commercial enterprises. He married Sarah Luzette Voss. Their children included two daughters who married well-known Kernersville physicians—Birdie Luola to Dr. Walter Clark Ashworth and Zora Bessie to Dr. John Robert Paddison—while another daughter, Eva Maud, married James Frederick Kerner.

Jesse Washington Sapp was a successful farmer who lived in the Deep River area of Guilford County, just a short distance east of Kernersville. Born on August 16, 1840, he later married Mahala Ballard, daughter of Jonathan Ballard Sr. Their children included a daughter named Mahala Cordelia, who was born January 26, 1869, and was likely named after her mother. An ugly incident that occurred on August 22, 1887, would forever mar the life of this young girl.

A hint of what happened found its way into print on August 24, 1887, when the *Greensboro Morning News* trumpeted the provocative headline: "RAPE! A Negro Fiend Commits an Outrage Upon a Young Lady at Kernersville!" According to the account, early the previous morning a startling rumor began circulating on the streets of Greensboro that "a railroad man who had just come in on a tricycle, from a trip up the Winston railroad, reported that he had seen an excited crowd in Kernersville who were about to lynch a negro man." When the railroad man inquired further, he "was informed that the negro had, by holding a pistol to her head and choking her almost to death, committed a horrible outrage upon the person of Miss Sapp, a beautiful and accomplished young lady, who is about 17 years of age." The paper added that it was believed the victim was a daughter of Mr. Jesse Sapp, "who lives just four miles this side of Kernersville."

A second report appeared in the same paper that day. It noted that since the previous story had been written, the "Winston train has arrived and the report, as to the outrage, is confirmed." It was also reported that "the officers of the law succeeded in getting the negro, Rufe [*sic*] Hairston, away from the mob and on board the train, and he is now in jail in this city." According to other information in the story, it seems that even though "the negro used the pistol and choked the lady and wounded her severely he did not accomplish his purpose, her cries bringing her father, who arrived in time to recognize the negro and see him run away." The piece confirmed that a crowd had in fact gathered at Kernersville, and its members were described as "frantic with rage." Perhaps more ominously, the report stated that "persons who came down with the prisoner said it was openly declared by the leaders of the mob that they would come on to Greensboro and hang the negro before the dawn of day."

The narrative concluded, "When we closed our office at a later hour the arrival of the mob was momentarily expected."

As the paper correctly anticipated, sometime between two and three o'clock in the morning, after the *Morning News* had gone to press, a crowd of some fifty masked men rode into Greensboro on horses and mules. Details were carried in a special edition of the *Morning News* on the morning of August 25, 1887, and were headlined with one word: "Lynched!"

According to the paper, the men came into the city by way of the High Point Road. Given the intense state of unrest in Kernersville over the attack, it seems likely that many came from that town and the surrounding area. Oliver L. Stafford of Kernersville, in an interview printed in the November 12, 1970 issue of the *Kernersville News*, recalled the incident. He was about nine years old at the time it took place. Stafford mentioned "the night a lynch mob on horseback stopped by his house on the way to Greensboro to break a man out of jail." According to his recollection,

"They brought him back and hung him where the big oaks are on Spring Garden Road. Then they rode round and round and shot him full of holes." At the time of the incident, Stafford's family lived on a farm just off the old Greensboro Road, the probable route the men took to Greensboro.

Once in Greensboro, the crowd of armed men proceeded directly to the jail, where Hairston was being held. They demanded that the jailer turn the prisoner over. The jailer resisted, but the insistent mob brushed him aside and used sledgehammers and crowbars to batter down the door of Hairston's cell. After pulling him out, the men tied him up with ropes and, with the hapless prisoner in tow, proceeded to the suburbs. There, in the vicinity of the Jackson farm, Hairston was hanged from a tree; it is said there was a little brick schoolhouse close by. According to the account in the paper:

> *The whole thing was done very quietly. He was given a few minutes to pray which he did very earnestly, and confessed his guilt. When seen this morning hanging by the neck from the limb of a tree, he was in his shirt sleeves and had his hat folded up and stuck in his pants pocket. His body was riddled with bullets and a card pinned upon his breast was so badly cut up that it could not be read.*

After completing their deadly work, the masked men left Greensboro and dispersed back to their homes.

Not surprisingly, the *Kernersville News*, a paper published every Thursday, carried an expanded account of this dreadful business. While that edition of the *News* no longer exists, a copy of its contents can still be found in the September 1, 1887 edition of the *Greensboro North State*. According to this narrative:

> *The neighborhood around Colfax was thrown into great excitement last Tuesday morning over the report that an outrage had been committed upon Miss Mahala C. Sapp, daughter of Jesse W. Sapp, by a negro, and soon a body of men, well armed, were in search of the scoundrel.*
>
> *Miss Sapp is of good family, quiet in demeanor and lady-like in all her deportment, and when the particulars of the deed spread, the whole community became thoroughly aroused, and it was believed that in the event the negro was caught he would be hung at once.*

It seems that Miss Sapp, about seventeen years of age but strong and healthy, had walked to her grandmother's carrying some milk. She left her grandmother's house about half past ten o'clock in the morning to return home. Apparently, only a short distance from where her grandmother lived, the road left the main road to Greensboro and wound its way through a wooded area to her home. "As she turned off to the right, she noticed a negro coming down the main road, but supposing he was going down towards Greensboro thought nothing of it." She was passing through the woods when the same Negro jumped out by her side. Again according to the Kernersville paper:

> *He grabbed her fiercely by the arm, and when she resisted, threw her to the ground, choking her savagely to stop her screams and threatened her life with the pistol which he presented unless she yielded to his request. She was too strong for him and continued to scream and use her strength in defense of her virtue. After a scuffle lasting from five to ten minutes, he released her, again threatening to shoot her, and without accompanying* [sic] *his fiendish designs, ran off through the woods.*

Her father and some others, upon hearing her screams, came running, but by that time the assailant had run off into the woods. They "found her greatly exhausted, and with her throat, breast and face badly bruised and scratched."

Upon questioning the young girl, they obtained a description of the Negro, and as the paper put it, "it was no trouble to recognize Jean Hairston as the guilty party as soon as he was met by a party going from Kernersville to the neighborhood in which the deed was done." Hairston, when confronted, was asked where he had been. He answered that he had "only been down to Pomp Rights," a man who lived just on the edge of Kernersville. But the members of the party made further inquiry as they drove along the road toward Colfax, and from the answers they received from those they met, they determined that Hairston had actually been several miles farther east than he claimed. This immediately cast him under suspicion.

According to the paper, "This suspicion was increased to a positive conviction when they learned the description furnished by Miss Sapp, and the party at once returned to town and surrounded Sophia Hairston's house," where Eugene was hiding. But when the officer entered the house to arrest him, Hairston "jumped out the window and began to run." He was quickly caught and "carried before Squire Sechrest at Colfax, who was assisted by Squire J.M. Guyer, of this place [Kernersville]," both men being justices of the peace. The account in the paper continued:

> *The evidence against him proved the guilt beyond a single doubt. The lady had described him accurately—nothing was missing. As soon as she saw him, she at once recognized him as the guilty party, and swore positively to his being the right person. Mr. Ballard had seen a negro walking the road about twenty steps behind Miss Sapp, and upon oath stated that Hairston was the negro. The red mud on his pants, his effort to escape, the evidence in full, made his guilt unquestionable.*

At this point, Hairston was bound over to court for trial and brought by Officer Will Gamble back to Kernersville, where the plan was to transport him to Greensboro by the next train. However, while he was being held in jail, an angry crowd began to assemble, and soon there was talk of preventing his reaching Greensboro at all. Recognizing the growing seriousness of the situation, Gamble slipped Hairston from his cell and "hurried off to Friendship with him in a buggy, there taking the train to Greensboro." The community of Friendship in Guilford County is where Piedmont Triad International Airport is located today.

A further account of this matter appeared in the *Greensboro Morning News* of August 26, 1887, including an account of the testimony of Miss Mahala Sapp before Justice of the Peace Sechrest, and proceedings of a coroner's jury convened to examine the hanging. The paper stated that "believing that the public would be interested in reading the sworn evidence of Miss Mahala C. Sapp, before the Justice of the Peace who issued the warrant for the arrest of Eugene Hairston, on the charge of making a criminal assault upon that lady, we append the following, which we find on file in the office of the clerk of the Superior Court." The paper then inserted the following:

> *NORTH CAROLINA, Guilford County*
> *State vs. Eugene Hairston—Before S.W. Sechrest, J.P.*
> *Warrant for an Assault and an Attempt to commit Rape*
>
> *Mahala C. Sapp, being duly sworn, complains and says that at and in the county aforesaid and in Deep River Township, on or about the 22d day of August 1887, Eugene Hairston did unlawfully and willfully assault the body of the said complainant and did attempt to commit rape on her person, against the form of the Statute and contrary to law, and against the peace and Dignity of the State.*

The sworn statement of Mahala Cordelia Sapp, subscribed and sworn at a preliminary examination before S.W. Sechrest, justice of the peace, on August 23, 1887, followed next, her testimony being as follows:

> *She was going home from her grandmother's, and as she came to the railroad crossing, she saw a colored man coming down the railroad. She crossed the railroad and went on towards home and the defendant, Eugene Hairston, followed her, and passing her, went on a piece further and stopped by the road-side. When she came up he asked her whose daughter she was and where she lived. She told him. He then asked her if she wanted 50 cents. She told him no. He then took hold of her and throwing her down, choked her. She commenced screaming. He said, "If you don't hush I'll shoot you," and drew a pistol—but did not shoot. He then left her. Her throat was considerable scratched up.*

At the hearing, there was also testimony by Jasper N. Hull, who lived in the vicinity of Colfax at the time of the incident. He stated that

> *he was working in his tobacco and Mahala C. Sapp passed by him, and the defendant, Eugene Hairston, was about twenty-five or thirty steps behind her. He saw him catch up with her and soon they got under the hill out of sight. Then he heard a woman screaming and started in a run to see what was the matter, but did not get there before the screaming stopped. He did not see the defendant then.*

Following the statements by Sapp and Hull at the preliminary examination, Eugene Hairston, the defendant, insisted on making a statement himself, which was allowed:

> *He said that he came to Pomp Writs* [sic], *about one and a half miles this side of Kernersville, and did not come any further down the railroad, and that he never saw Mahala C. Sapp before he saw her at her father's house after he was arrested and taken there.*

The final witness at the preliminary examination of Hairston was James Ballard, a brother to Mahala C. Sapp's mother. In his affidavit, he said that "he overtook Eugene Hairston, going up the railroad, from three-quarters to one mile this side of where he said he was, and he seemed to be somewhat uneasy."

The August 26, 1887 edition of the *Greensboro Morning News* also carried an account of a coroner's jury summoned to hear evidence. Guilford County coroner A.N. Hinton summoned several individuals "for the purpose of holding an inquest over the dead body" of Eugene Hairston. Jurors summoned were Yancey Clark, F. Detmering, D.A. Whitsell, J.F. Shaw, Hiram Lindsay and Jerry Grasty. The group assembled about 10:30 a.m. at the location where Hairston's body was still hanging from a tree. They lowered it to the ground and conducted an examination, which revealed that "besides having been hung by the neck, his body had been pierced by many buck shot and bullets." In fact, the investigation yielded no further information other than the fact that Hairston's death had come "at the hands of a masked mob."

The jury was about to render this verdict when a group of colored men, also gathered there, "expressed the belief that the perpetrators could be discovered if the proper efforts were made on the part of the coroner." After further consultation, Coroner Hinton ordered the case adjourned "to a further day to await developments." According to the paper, the jury was adjourned to meet again on the following Saturday, September 3, 1887. Whether in fact the jury reconvened—and if it did, what it concluded—has not been determined, as no further relevant newspaper accounts have been located. It does seem doubtful that any members of the lynch mob were ever taken into custody. It was reported, however, that the coroner remarked to the *Morning News* reporter that he was sure of one thing and that was "that the man who tied the knot knew his business thoroughly."

The story concluded with the report that "Hairston's step-father and mother, and his sister, came to the city yesterday with a one-horse wagon and left about 4 o'clock carrying with them the corpse" for burial in Kernersville.

The *Greensboro North State* of September 1, 1887, ran a further narrative of the Hairston lynching. It noted that Squire Sechrest, the justice of the peace before whom Hairston had a preliminary examination, had come to Greensboro on the previous Monday (August 29) and while there said that "the young lady did not swear positively that the prisoner was the man who assaulted her," although she said that "to the best of her belief he was the man."

The paper added that people from all over the county had been in Greensboro following the lynching, and it was the general opinion there that "no one regretted the punishment the man received." The paper then enunciated what it believed to be the prevailing belief among the populace:

> *The general feeling seems to be that in all such cases where the man is caught, and the identity and commission of the offense are unquestionable that the brute ought to be killed on the spot. But that after the friends of the assailed and the people in the neighborhood allow the party to become a prisoner and while he is in the custody of the law, no mob should be allowed to outrage the law by taking him from the jail.*

The paper then severely criticized what it called the "apparent helplessness of our officers," referring to the law enforcement authorities who allowed Hairston to fall into the hands of the mob. The article then lamented, "Where is the safety of our citizens if the town can be invaded at midnight and handled as if our sentinels were chloroformed?"

Despite its concerns over lawlessness, the paper seemed inclined to agree with the sentiments of the population at large:

> *Our women must be protected above all things. They are our most precious jewels, and earthly happiness is dependent upon their purity and inviolability. When their virtue is assailed let the actual or would-*

> *be ravisher, when he is caught and identified, be killed on the spot like a wild beast if it can be done before the law lays its hands on him.*

On the other hand, it added that once a person has been apprehended by proper officials, the law should be allowed to take its proper course, meaning that Hairston should have been tried, not lynched. The paper concluded:

> *The law is the power of the people, and the officers who quietly stand by and see it violated and treated with contempt not only are guilty of criminal negligence, but they are contributing to the cultivation of a reckless and lawless sentiment which will in time sap the foundation of all society. Both church and State become weak in the eyes of the people who can safely defy the law of the land.*

The Winston-Salem papers also weighed in with a full story of the attack and lynching that appeared in the *People's Press* of September 1, 1887. Called "Horrible Crime," the story characterized the attack as a "most diabolical outrage" and postulated that, had not Mahala Sapp's father and several others come to her rescue, "she would have been murdered." While describing the lynching scene, the paper noted that,

> *when seen this morning, hanging by his neck from the limb of a tree,* [Hairston] *was in his shirt sleeves, and had his hat folded up and struck in his pants' pocket. His body was riddled with bullets, and a playing card, "the ten of hearts," pinned upon his breast was so badly cut up that it could not be read.*

The paper went on to state that "various rumors of plots among the negroes were current, but so far nothing has been done."

One last word regarding the Hairston episode appeared in an issue of the *Kernersville News* that is also now missing. It was, however, reprinted in the September 8, 1887 issue of the *People's Press*:

> *Everything is now quiet after the lynching of Hairston. All right-thinking people, both white and black, agree that the punishment was well deserved and if the law had done less it would have failed in its duty to society. Let the matter rest here as a warning to evil doers, and not as an encouragement to mob violence.*

As for Mahala Cordelia Sapp, the record shows that she never married; instead, she spent the remainder of her life with family members in the Deep River area where she was born. She died there in 1933 and was buried in the churchyard of Shady Grove Wesleyan Church at Colfax.

While a dark episode, the entire Hairston matter was the only recorded lynching in Guilford County. Certainly, during the closing decades of the nineteenth century, the lynching of blacks in the South and in border states was commonly used to terrorize them and maintain white control. While most lynchings were by hanging or shooting—or both, as in the case of Eugene Hairston—many employed more hideous methods.

Lynching statistics have been kept since about 1882. Prior to that year, there are no reliable estimates. One of the most respected sources of information comes from Tuskegee University, which began keeping statistics in 1892. As expected, the data reveal that most people who were lynched were black, but certainly not all. Tuskegee data show that between 1882 and 1968, a total of 3,445 blacks were lynched compared to 1,297 whites.

There was at least one case in Forsyth County, North Carolina, that involved the lynching of a white man named Henry Swaim. An interesting account of this affair can be found in Jennifer Bean Bower's *Winston & Salem: Tales of Murder, Mystery and Mayhem.*

The evidence showed that Swaim attacked a lady named Ernestina Reid, cutting her throat and inflicting other blows that resulted in her death. Ernestina was the wife of farmer Harrison Reid, who lived in the Moravian community of Freidland, and both of the Reids were highly regarded around Salem.

Swaim was apprehended and lodged in the Forsyth County jail. As he was being escorted there, groups of infuriated citizens taunted him. Not long after being placed in a cell, an angry mob began to assemble. Forsyth County sheriff Augustus Fogle stepped outside to reason with them and eventually they dispersed. However, that same night, at about two o'clock, a group of masked men appeared and demanded the prisoner. Sheriff Fogle again tried to talk to them, but his efforts were to no avail. The mayor of Winston and the chief of police also arrived and attempted to calm the armed crowd, but they, too, failed. Eventually the mob had its way, taking Swaim in hand and tying his hands behind his back.

The mob marched Swaim through the streets of the adjoining town of Salem and then on to the top of a hill on the road to Waughtown where a large tree stood. Swaim was allowed to respond to several questions, during which time he admitted that he had killed Ernestina Reid and described how he had carried out the act. Following that confession, a rope was placed around his neck. He requested that someone say a short prayer for him, after which he was hoisted into the air and left to swing from the tree until dead. His body was left hanging until two o'clock the following afternoon, during which time it is estimated that thousands of people viewed it.

THE AFFRONT THAT TURNED DEADLY

As noted elsewhere, one of the many prominent members of the Sapp family of Kernersville was Benjamin Jackson Sapp, a well-known physician and druggist and also proprietor of the Sapp Hotel on the town square. This was the old stand that dated back to 1788, when it was called Dobson's Tavern.

Dr. Sapp and his wife, Delia Whittington, had two sons who became doctors. Carey C. Sapp studied dentistry and later practiced in Statesville, North Carolina. He is mentioned in a short item in the *Landmark* of Statesville, North Carolina, on March 31, 1887:

> *The Kernersville News of the 25th contains the following article: Mr. Cary C. Sapp, son of Dr. B.J. Sapp, returned from Maryland University with "blushing honors thick upon him." He took a high stand in his classes and graduated in dentistry among the very foremost. Out of a class of over fifty he was awarded a very handsome gold medal for best cohesive gold filling. After taking a course with Dr. C.J. Watkins, of Salem, spending a year at the Vanderbilt University and taking the degree of D.D.S. at Baltimore, he should be well equipped for his profession. He has decided to locate at Statesville, where we hope to hear of his continued success.*

The other son, Luther Lafayette Sapp, was born in Kernersville on October 16, 1868. After obtaining his MD from Jefferson Medical College in Philadelphia, he returned to Kernersville, where, like his father, he practiced medicine. On November 7, 1893, he married Penelope Creesy Fetter, called Nellie by her family and friends. The service was performed by Episcopal minister Reverend Alfred H. Stubbs, rector of St. Barnabas Church in Greensboro. Witnesses included his father, Dr. B.J. Sapp, J.N. Leak and J.W. Hasten.

Nellie was the daughter of Frederick Augustus Fetter and his wife, Mary C. Wright. According to Archibald Henderson's *North Carolina: The Old North State and the New*, Fetter was born at Flushing, Long Island, on November 9, 1838, and died on January 18, 1910. He received his BA in 1859 and his MA in 1862, both from the University of North Carolina. During the Civil War, he served as a lieutenant in the Confederate army and then took up teaching at the University of North Carolina, first as a tutor and then as an instructor. He later became a minister of the Episcopal Church. Another daughter of Reverend Frederick Fetter, Mary Augusta, also married a Kernersville man and first cousin to Luther Lafayette. He was Oscar LaMay Sapp, son of Newell Wesley Sapp of Kernersville. Oscar attended Kernersville Academy and then the University of North Carolina, where he obtained both his undergraduate and law degrees. He later became a prominent attorney in Greensboro.

Following their marriage in November 1893, Dr. Sapp and his lovely young bride Nellie must have looked forward to a lifetime of happiness together. However, their joy was soon to be interrupted by an ugly incident that would occur just a few weeks later, during the height of the festive season that surrounded Christmas. It involved a confrontation between Dr. Sapp and another Kernersville man named James Lamar. Lamar, born on September 18, 1873, was the son of George Lamar and his wife, Lacy Ann Jordan. He was also a twin brother of Eugene Lamar, whose shooting death in 1905 at the hands of Ade Walker is described in another story.

According to the January 4, 1894 edition of the *Union Republican*, a newspaper published in Winston-Salem, Dr. Sapp and Nellie attended a Christmas entertainment in Kernersville on Saturday night, December 23. Afterward, walking back to their own home, they encountered James Lamar on the street. It seems that Lamar was exceedingly rude and, according to the paper, addressed the couple "in some insulting language which so incensed Dr. Sapp that he without much ado knocked Lamar down." Following the exchange, Sapp and his wife proceeded home.

Later that same evening, Lamar showed up at the doctor's house and uttered some words of apology. However, he then endeavored to get Sapp to visit a patient. The doctor believed that Lamar's request was only a trick, so he declined.

The following morning, December 24, Dr. Sapp headed out to visit a patient. However, it appears that he met someone who informed him that he might expect an attack from Lamar, so he returned home and armed himself with a pistol. Some time after leaving home, Dr. Sapp once again

encountered Lamar, this time near the railroad depot in the north end of town.

During the ensuing confrontation, Lamar insisted on settling their difficulty, to which Sapp replied "that the trouble had been amicably adjusted the previous evening." At that point, Lamar grew angry and launched an assault on Sapp, "striking three or four times and reaching in his hip pocket as if to draw a pistol." Dr. Sapp, taking quick note of Lamar's actions, drew his own pistol and fired. According to the story, the ball lodged in Lamar's liver. Badly wounded but still conscious, Lamar immediately withdrew from the scene.

The town constable soon arrived, and Sapp was arrested and placed under a $1,000 bond pending trial, which he promptly gave. According to the paper, the preliminary hearing was deferred until Lamar's condition "takes a turn for the better or worse"; the paper speculated that "most probably it will be the latter."

The paper concluded by noting that Lamar, who was twenty years old, was said "to be possessed of a wild and reckless temperament." Dr. Sapp, on the other hand, was characterized as a well-known practicing physician, highly respected in the community.

Several days later, on January 10, 1894, the *Greensboro Patriot* reported that "James Lamar, the man who was shot in Kernersville by Dr. L.L. Sapp on December 24th," had in fact died. It also stated that Sapp's bond was set at $2,000. The *Patriot* did recite that the difficulty between Sapp and Lamar, whom the paper claimed "bore a bad reputation," originated over an insult to Mrs. Sapp.

On January 11, the *Union Republican* carried another update in which it noted that James Lamar had died of his wounds on Thursday night, January 4. The paper reiterated that the difficulty between the two men "originated over an insult to Mrs. Sapp while walking upon the street with her husband the evening before the shooting."

Following Lamar's death, Dr. Sapp was given a preliminary hearing in Kernersville on Tuesday the ninth, and it is said that it occupied the entire day. A number of witnesses were examined on both sides. Dr. Sapp was represented by lawyers Watson, Glenn and Bodenhamer. Watson and Glenn were very probably the prominent Winston-Salem attorneys Cyrus B. Watson and Robert B. Glenn, while Bodenhamer was likely W.M. Bodenhamer, a Kernersville attorney and son of Dr. Levi Bodenhamer. The lawyer for the state in the preliminary hearing was K.B. Jones. At the close of the hearing, Dr. Sapp was bound over to the superior court on $3,000 bond, which he gave, with his father, Dr. B.J. Sapp, N.S. Leak and C.T. Snider as sureties. The court was slated to convene in Winston-Salem on February 26.

On March 1, 1894, the *Union Republican* carried further news of the proceedings involving Sapp, which took place at Forsyth County Superior Court in Winston. Judge Spier Whitaker was the presiding judge. Judge Whitaker, born in Halifax County, North Carolina, was appointed to the position of superior court judge in 1889 by then governor Daniel G. Fowle.

The judge came up to Winston-Salem on the morning train from Greensboro and called the court to order about eleven o'clock. A number of grand jurors were drawn, and they included T.A. Crews, foreman; Samuel Vance; Samuel Whit; H.F. Hines; P.H. Stimpson; H.H. Long; H.H. Sink; J.F. Doub; J.M. Gordon; William Jarvis; J.M. Glasscock; R.L. Yarboro; N.A. Stedman; R.W. Davis; Wesley Idol; John E. Johnson; F.L. Ziglar; and H.T. Foucht.

Judge Whitaker seems to have been an interesting character because, as a preface to his charge to the jury, he went into an explanation regarding his tardiness in arriving at court. According to the paper:

> *His Honor stated that this was the second time since he had been on the Bench that he failed to be present and to open court promptly at 10 o'clock Monday—the other instance being at Taylorsville, Alexander county, both the delays being the result of late trains and failure to make railroad connections. He explained further that he had heretofore addressed the Grand Jury extempore, his training being such as to enable him to do so intelligently, but on this occasion he had written out his charge in full and any Grand Juror, member of the bar or newspaper representative who wished to refer to it was welcome so to do.*

The paper, citing "the 'reputation' the Judge has made elsewhere as set forth by a number of Newspapers of the District, as well as the general interest that must necessarily center in such a document," availed itself of the judge's offer and reprinted the charge in full. However, it is omitted here as it had little to do with the Sapp case.

The judge next turned his attention to the cold weather outside and the poor condition of the room itself. For one thing, he "very pleasantly but pointedly suggested that as the broken window panes near his chair were certain death, they would be promptly repaired." The judge, it seems, had few comments about the courthouse itself, but the reporter for the paper suggested that he was "no doubt surprised at the lack of public spirit for so progressive a town and section and doubtless feels the discomfort of the totally inadequate quarters" he was given.

Finally, on Monday evening, after what was surely a long day, "the Grand Jury returned a true bill against Dr. L.L. Sapp, for the murder of James Lamar, at Kernersville, last December." Then, a jury was drawn from a special panel of fifty prospective jurors. According to the last report, "the case was taken up yesterday and it is believed it will occupy several days." The attorneys selected to defend Sapp were Watson & Ruxton and Glenn & Manly, while a man called Solicitor Berber and E.B. Jones were to be the prosecutors for the state.

Oddly, despite the extensive coverage, no further mention of the outcome of Sapp's trial appears in either the Winston-Salem or Greensboro papers. It seems likely, however, that Sapp was either found innocent on the grounds of self-defense or given a light sentence at best. Perhaps some further information regarding the outcome of the trial will yet surface.

In any case, following the trial, Dr. Sapp and Nellie moved to Reidsville, North Carolina, where he resumed his medical practice and also operated a drugstore. Later it seems that he left Reidsville because in 1910 the Sapp family was residing in the town of Edenton in Chowan County. How long they remained there is unclear because, by 1930, they were living in Albemarle, in Stanley County.

It is not known when Sapp's wife, Nellie, died. It is known, however, that the doctor himself died in Portsmouth, Virginia, in 1933, as indicated by the following obituary that appeared in the *Virginian Pilot & Norfolk Landmark* on Thursday, April 6, 1933:

> *Sapp, Luther L. M.D.—In the residence of his daughter, Mrs. T. Sanford Cocke, 718 Court street, Portsmouth, Va., Wednesday morning, April 5, 1933 at 11:35 o'clock, Luther L. Sapp, M.D., age 64 years. Remains will be forwarded by Southern Railway this* [Thursday] *evening at 7:35 o'clock to Reidsville, N.C. for funeral services and interment.*

It seems that years later one Kernersville citizen, Oliver L. Stafford, still recalled the shooting that killed James Lamar and mentioned it to Marg Going, a reporter for the *Kernersville News*, during an interview in 1970. Stafford was then ninety-three years old. Going published her story in the November 12, 1970 edition of the paper. Stafford said he remembered "a husband killing the man who had insulted his wife" and then added, "She was awful good looking."

Following his death in January 1894, James Lamar was buried in the Crews-Dwiggins Cemetery about three miles from Kernersville. His twin brother, Eugene, would join him there in August 1905 after being shot to death by Ade Walker in a drunken quarrel in Granville Manuel's blacksmith shop, almost certainly close to the location where Dr. Sapp fired the bullet that ended James's life.

A DEADLY SHOOTOUT WITH REVENUE OFFICERS

On December 21, 1959, the *People's News*, a Kernersville paper, carried an interview with longtime town resident George P. Winfree. Born in Kernersville on May 3, 1885, he was the son of William Franklin and Josephine Oakes Winfree. The main focus of the interview, conducted by the newspaper's editor, Paul J. "Pete" Nash Jr., was a man named Banner Jordan, called by Winfree "Kernersville's most feared man."

As told by Winfree, in the early 1890s Kernersville "was a pretty rough town and was the talk throughout the entire state of North Carolina." In fact, he claimed that "it was not safe to be on the streets." This was especially the case at night, as there were no streetlights, but only twenty-three old oil lamps lining Main Street from the old Southern Railway depot to the Kernersville Moravian Church. The lamplighter in those days was a youth named John M. Pinnix, who, in 1904, would establish a well-known drugstore on the town square and become known as "Neighbor" Pinnix. In order to light the lamps, Pinnix had to carry a ladder on his rounds. For his lamplighting efforts, he was paid three dollars each month, big money at that time. According to Winfree, some of the rougher characters in town used to shoot out the lamps—sometimes even as the lamplighter was struggling to light them. As Winfree put it, "This was the day of Banner Jordan, Wick Walker, Ade Walker and others who demanded respect and got it, too."

Banner Jordan was George Banner Jordan. Born in Kernersville on August 8, 1867, he was the son of Robert A. "Bob" Jordan and Minerva Ballard. According to Winfree, Bob Jordan "was a good man at heart, however he meant business and so did his son Banner. They would often help needy people. Those that had no money would come to the Jordans for help and they got it always."

A horse trader, Bob Jordan had for many years operated a livery stable on the north side of Bodenhamer Street, just across from where the old train depot stands today. This stable later became one of the warehouses for the Cash Feed Store operated by Kenneth Greenfield, and the building still stands. An 1888 book by Dr. D.P. Robbins called *A Descriptive Sketch of Winston-Salem* included a sketch of Kernersville that mentions the stable:

> *This business comes neither under merchandise or manufacturing, but is yet important to any progressive village. R.A. Jordan is a native of the place, and owns quite a large number of lots in the village, which can be bought for improvement at low figures. He has been for nine years past in the livery business, and keeps all kinds of stock and turnouts necessary for the accommodation of the people who desire livery hire.*

The Jordan homeplace was located just up the road from the livery stable and formerly stood on a lot located between Bodenhamer and King Streets, just north of present-day Winfree Street. James R. Winfree, a former Kernersville resident who grew up on King Street close to the location of the Jordan home and was a relation of George P. Winfree, provided the following description:

> *The Jordan house was a very large two story house with a huge attic on Bodenhamer Street. If you are coming from Greensboro and take Bodenhamer St. to Winfree Street, which is on the right, going toward Main St., The house sat far off the street with lots of Oak trees about a half block past Winfree. When they tore the house down, they built two small houses from the lumber. I remember being in one of those houses. My aunt lived in one and they would point out a knot hole in the wall and say that that was from one of the bullets that killed Banner Jordan. We could sit for hours and study that knot hole.*

Banner Jordan also dealt in illicit whiskey. In those days, such men were often called "blockaders," their business was termed "blockading" and their product was widely known as blockade whiskey, or just "blockade." It seems that his father, too, dabbled in this illegal commerce from time to time. A piece in the March 11, 1896 edition of the *Greensboro Patriot* put it this way: "Robert Jordan was not looked upon as being a particularly bad man, although he too was known to have a weakness for dealing in moonshine liquor."

According to George P. Winfree's recollections, Banner was loyal to those he considered his friends and would even risk his life for them, as he feared no man. But if he did not like you, that was an entirely different matter. He carried two guns on his hip at all times, and many considered him not only the fastest draw around but a good shot too.

Despite his constant flouting of the law, it seems that none of the police officers in Kernersville dared to arrest Banner or even serve a warrant on him; that is, until one day when he was confronted by a constable named Frank Linville. Here is the story as told by Winfree to Nash:

> *Frank liked the Jordans but* [there] *came a day when he had to serve a warrant on Banner and Frank did not want to. But he went to Banner's home and told Banner to come out peacefully as he had a warrant for him. Banner replied, "You are not going to serve it Frank. Don't come any closer. I don't want to kill you." Frank did, and they shot it out on the street, neither hitting the other and finally Frank walked off and said to Banner, "I did not want to arrest you anyway. Go in the house, Banner, and don't give me any more trouble."*

Given the fact that Banner was a good shot, it seems likely that he had no real desire to wound or kill Linville, and the same could probably be said of the other man.

Frank Linville wasn't the only policeman to have trouble with Banner and his friends, brothers Ade and Wick Walker. Another was Will Gamble, who succeeded Linville in the job. Again, according to Winfree:

> *One day Banner sent Ade up town to get some groceries. Will Gamble, policeman, had a warrant for Ade and grabbed him by the coat but Ade pulled away leaving his coat. He went back and told Banner that Will Gamble had tried to arrest him and he had his coat. Banner told Ade to go back and tell Will to give him his coat back and if he did not he would come and get it. Ade did this and came right back with his coat.*

Wick Walker was the wagon driver for Banner Jordan and helped transport the blockade whiskey. According to George P. Winfree, one day

> *Banner and Wick were hauling liquor in a wagon. Wick saw two revenue officers, Walt Davis and Jim Smith, coming toward them on horseback. Banner was in the bottom of the wagon asleep. Wick woke Banner and said the revenue officers were coming. Banner replied, "I will take care of them boys." He pulled out two guns and they turned away and ran and Banner shot the dust from under the horses' feet.*

Davis and Smith were no doubt incensed by this ill treatment and likely vowed revenge—a vow they honored.

While some of George P. Winfree's recollections may be a bit embroidered, it's clear that Banner Jordan was a dangerous character, all too willing to shoot men who crossed him. This claim is substantiated by a short notice in the May 11, 1893 edition of the *Landmark*, a newspaper published in Statesville, North Carolina, which reads: "Banner Jordan, a desperate character, shot Lute Hester and Yancey Linville through their right hands during a row at Kernersville, Forsyth county, Thursday night of last week." Not only that, but the previously mentioned March 11, 1896 edition of the *Greensboro Patriot* noted that a

> *few years earlier, Banner was charged with an attempt to murder a man in Randolph County whom he believed had informed on him for retailing* [whiskey], *and he was considered an outlaw,* [and that] *it was only last week that his father finished paying off his forfeited bond of $2,000.*

Following his failure to appear for trial in regard to the attempted murder in Randolph, and his subsequent designation as an outlaw, Banner's further visits to his father's home were necessarily surreptitious. Events were starting to creep up on Banner, events that culminated in a deadly shootout with revenue officers Walt Davis and Jim Smith on one cold March morning in 1896.

One of the first newspapers to depict the encounter between Banner Jordan and his father and the two revenue officers was the March 10, 1896 edition of the *Landmark* in Statesville, which blared the following headline: "Killed by Revenue Officers: Bob and Banner Jordan Meet Death at the Hands of Revenue Officers Davis and Smith." The story was originally a special from Winston to the *Charlotte Observer*.

According to the brief account of the events that transpired that fateful day, the fight broke out about 7:10 a.m. at Bob Jordan's home and "was a battle royal for a few minutes." The revenue officers had traveled to the Jordan home in search of blockade whiskey. Finding a keg hidden in a woodpile, the officers entered the home and were upstairs hunting for more whiskey when Banner, hiding in the attic, fired on Davis, shooting off his finger. After Banner fired a second time, "Davis told Smith that he was badly hurt." As Smith was helping his wounded partner back down the stairs, Bob Jordan appeared and began firing. As the story has it, "Davis drew his pistol and shot over Smith's shoulder, putting four balls in the father, killing him

almost instantly." During the time the shooting was going on upstairs, the officers "shot Banner four times, causing him to fall from the garret to the second floor." Later, as the officers were leaving the house, "Banner crawled to a window and shot at them."

The story continues by noting that officers Davis and Smith "are under arrest at Greensboro and were not able to be brought back to Kernersville for preliminary trial." While the Jordans were both dead, the two officers had also sustained serious injuries. According to the account, "All the muscles of Smith's left arm are shot off. Davis was shot by Banner in the groin besides in one hand." Ironically, the two revenue officers, both from Stokes County, were, until a few years earlier, blockaders themselves.

The story concludes:

> *Banner, the son, has had a bad reputation for several years and was regarded by many people as an outlaw. A man who was at Jordan's house*

> *several days ago is quoted as saying that he saw thirteen guns standing in one corner. Banner said he kept them there to protect himself from revenue officers. Banner told his physician this morning that if the Lord would spare him this time he would lead a different life. He died at 10 o'clock.*

A more detailed version of the shootout soon followed in the March 12, 1896 edition of the *Union Republican* in Winston. Headlined as a "Fatal Shooting Affair," this account is reproduced below in its entirety. It contains a somewhat different version of events:

> *There was more excitement in Kernersville Monday morning to the square inch, than at any previous time in the history of that town "and old corn liquor was the cause of it all." The origin was a shooting unto death of Rob't and Banner Jordan, father and son, by revenue officers James Smith and Walter Davis, while the latter carry wounds that will mark them for life. From many accounts of the affair we subjoin the following report:*
>
> *On Sunday, owing to information received at the Revenue office in Greensboro, necessary papers were made out and officers James Smith and Walter Davis took the night train to Kernersville. Officers Whittington and Tate also started for the same point in private conveyance.*
>
> *Early Monday morning Messrs. Smith and Davis went to residence of Rob't Jordan, near the rail road depot and searching around the yard found a barrel of liquor hidden in the wood pile. The elder Jordan was "Not at Home" when called for, but appeared after the liquor had been found and upon request to search his house, assented and accompanied the officers. On the first and second floors nothing was found, but noticing a trap door leading to an attic, officer Davis started up and had reached the door when someone fired at him from above, the ball hitting Davis on the right wrist and he fell to the floor. As there was no flooring in the attic, Banner Jordan, the son, who fired the shot, must have missed his footing, for he came with a crash through the ceiling and landing near Davis, when he fired again, this time the ball hitting Davis in the thigh, whereupon Davis returned the compliment, shooting Banner Jordan fatally, the ball passing through him and also wounding him in the arm. Just at this juncture the elder Jordan opened fire with a shotgun at Smith from below, hitting him, or rather sprinkling him severely on the arm and body with shot. Either Smith or Davis returned the fire and killed Rob't Jordan at the first shot. The fusillade occurred in so short a space of time and under such excitement that a really accurate version is difficult for even the surviving participants to narrate.*

> *The difficulty took place about sunup and Banner Jordan lived until about 10:30 o'clock. Officers Whittington and Tate were not present, but were looking for spoils on the premises of a neighbor. The officers took the train for Greensboro and put up at the McAdoo House where Drs. Tate and Michaux dressed their wounds. The ball in the hand of Davis was extracted but the one in his thigh was not removed at once. Smith was filled with shot some of which were picked out.*
>
> *Officers Smith and Davis are from Stokes county and are said to have been blockaders at one time themselves. They are "grit," and so were the Jordans. It was "Greek meet Greek."*
>
> *Sympathy is duly extended to the wife and children of Rob't. Jordan. Of him it is said that he was a quiet man, but would engage in blockading. Banner, his son, was looked upon as a desperate character and at one time was outlawed, and had proven a deal of trouble and expense to his father, and finally caused the death of both.*
>
> *The officers are not able to be removed, but will give bond in Greensboro, or be placed under guard until they are able to appear for trial.*
>
> *The facts of the case are such that a Coroners' Inquest was not held.*
>
> *Tuesday the remains of Robert and Banner Jordan were interred in the Dwiggins graveyard a short distance from Kernersville.*
>
> *While the officers were in the discharge of their duty, it was a deplorable affair, and a warning to those who are tempted to evade the law.*

This same edition of the *Union Republican* carried a further description of events, which the paper characterized as "direct information as gathered by a citizen, who hearing of the affair, went immediately to the scene." According to this report, Smith and Davis went to the Jordan home and were invited inside. It was only after they "entered and had thus gained admittance to the house" that they informed Jordan "that the house was reported and added that they had no search warrant." It appears that Jordan told them to go ahead and search, and even accompanied them through the rooms on the lower floor. The officers then went to the second floor, but it seems Bob Jordan remained downstairs. When a search of the second floor also failed to disclose any whiskey, one of the officers asked Jordan about access to the attic. Banner Jordan was hiding in the attic, and "the Officers discerned him through a scuttle hole and he, Banner, told them he would come down. He started, but in some way caught in the ceiling by the arm, during which time the officers were shooting at him." Then, according to this account, Bob Jordan "asked the officers to cease their shooting in his house, but instead of complying they shot at him also. The shooting was effective and Bob Jordan closed his arms in a painful manner. He managed to get his doubled barreled shotgun and directing one load at one of the officers, fell back dead upon the floor." This piece concluded by noting that "the two officers have been leading blockaders and that their reputation has not been very good."

George P. Winfree, who lived in a house only a stone's throw from the Jordan home, has his own account. Its accuracy cannot be determined, but it does provide a good deal of colorful context. According to Winfree, on the Saturday preceding the Monday morning gunfight, a spy came to town and visited Bob Jordan at his home. The story continues:

> *Mr. Jordan had faith and confidence and trusted this man. The spy told Mr. Jordan that if he had any liquor in his home he had better hide it as a team had been seized at Beeson's Cross Road. Mr. Jordan told this man he had some liquor and he and the spy hid the liquor under a large woodpile. The spy remained around a while then left. Mr. Billy Winfree, a friend of the Jordans, whose barn was across the street from the Jordan's home, had his colored man hook up a team of horses and drove to Beeson's Cross Road to see if this was true and found out that no team had been seized. Mr. Billy Winfree told Bob Jordan that the man who came to see him was a spy and he better get the liquor away and his son too. The Winfrees owned the Foy place one mile down the Greensboro Road where the Pilgrim Bible College is today. Bob Rumley and a hired man lived there with him, Frank Christopher. Frank looked up the spy and beat him up. Frank was a large man about the same size as Banner Jordan and the spy took Frank to be Banner. He reported to the revenue officers that Banner had beat him up. On Sunday night, March the 8th, the revenue officers came to Kernersville in a hack. They camped and spent the night near the railroad tracks where the Mirawall* [sic: Mirawal] *plant is today. There were four of them and two remained with the hack. It was a cold March night and they built a fire. Monday morning, March the 9th, 6 a.m., Walt Davis and Jim Smith, revenue officers, came to the back of the Winfree home which was directly in front of the Jordan home. Mr. Winfree was in his yard and they told him that they wanted to search his barn. Mr. Billy said go right ahead. The barn was searched and when the revenue officers returned, Mr. Billy asked them if they had found anything. They said only a one armed man, Harp Jon, who was in the hayloft, who was selling liquor for a living that he had in a lock box. They said they bought two drinks and paid him a quarter a drink. The revenue officers then went to the home of Bob Jordan in search*

> *of Banner. Jim Smith and Walt Davis, revenue officers, went in the front door. Banner was in the attic of his house and missed his step on a wood joist and fell through the ceiling, hanging by his ankles. Jim Smith placed eight bullets into Banner. Walter Davis was at the head of the stairs at the hall when Jordan came out of his room at the foot of the stairway, with gun in his hand, and Walt Davis shot him through the heart.*

As might well be expected, a crowd soon converged on the site of the shooting. According to Winfree, he and his mother were the first present, and he reported that everyone came out of the Jordan home screaming. "The revenue officers came out with their guns in their hand and told everyone there to 'shut up or they would get more of the same.'"

Among the others on the scene that day was Kernersville resident Oliver L. Stafford, called "Nin" by everyone who knew him. He was ninety-three years old when he was interviewed by the *Kernersville News*; the story appeared in the November 12, 1970 edition under the headline: "Kernersville's Oldest Citizen Recalls History of Violence of Another Time." Stafford recalled that

> *when the revenuers came from Greensboro to search the house and arrest the men for beating one of their spies, the son hid in the attic. He opened fire on the searchers shooting off a finger of one of them.*
>
> *When they shot him he fell through the attic and landed beside his daddy on the bed. He was still alive when I got there. He asked if they had killed his dad, then he died.*

Despite these various and somewhat conflicting accounts, it seems likely that the two revenue officers entered the Jordan house without a search warrant. The March 11, 1896 edition of the *Greensboro Patriot* carried an account of the shooting, which claimed that

> *for some time it has been understood that Robert Jordan and his son Bannister, better known as Banner Jordan, living at Kernersville, nineteen miles west of this city, were handling blockade whisky, and it was to investigate the truth of well founded rumors to that effect that Deputy Collectors Walter F. Davis and Jas. S. Smith, of the agency in this city, were ordered to Kernersville Sunday night by-rail. Deputy Collector Tate and Mr. R.L. Whittington, armed with a search warrant for the Jordan premises, drove through in a private conveyance, reaching the scene just after hostilities had ceased.*

Based on this, it appears that the fighting was already over by the time Officer Whittington arrived with a search warrant. The story does claim that the officers received permission to search the house, but whether this is accurate cannot be ascertained. In this version of events, one of the officers noticed an attic

> *loosely covered with rough boards and Davis started up there to look around…and Davis had proceed far enough up to see two barrels of liquor there when he was shot twice in rapid succession by some one in the attic, his hand stopping a bullet that would have penetrated his brain had it not met with an obstruction.*

The *Patriot*'s description was not especially generous to Bob Jordan, noting that

> *while the shooting was going on deputy Smith stood at the head of the stairs and it was there old man Jordan opened fire on him with a shotgun, filling his right arm and side with bird shot. Almost in an instant the old man lay a corpse, having received a bullet that ended his career before he could execute his murderous design.*

It is clear that following the shootout Davis and Smith were taken by train to Greensboro, where their wounds were treated. None of them appeared life-threatening, although some thought that Davis might lose the finger that had been shattered in the deadly exchange.

This story also reported that a large crowd soon converged on the Jordan home: "The excitement at the scene of the shooting was intense, a crowd gathering on short order, but there was no disposition to make further trouble for the deputies." A deputy sheriff who arrived on the scene wanted to detain the two revenue officers, but he was persuaded instead to accompany them to Greensboro, where he could keep them "under surveillance" until Forsyth County sheriff McArthur could arrive. He did so on the next train, carrying with him warrants for their arrest, "which he left with Sheriff Hoskins, and they are now practically under his care." This was Joseph A. Hoskins, who was sheriff of Guilford County from 1894 to 1898.

The paper concluded with the following conjecture: "It is the general opinion that if the deputies had been able to remain for the coroner's inquest they would have been acquitted on the ground of justifiable homicide." In any event, both men were charged, and according to an account in the

March 26, 1896 edition of the *Union Republican*, both officers were

> *brought up from Greensboro, Tuesday, and given a preliminary examination in this city* [Winston]. *They were bound over to Forsyth Court in a $500 bond which they gave and left on the Norfolk & Western train for Stokes County, where both reside. The surety of officer Smith was Jackson Smith, an uncle, and of Officer Davis, J.W. Davis, his father.*

Regardless of the backgrounds of Bob Jordan and his son Banner, it appears that a significant element in the town of Kernersville believed it was wrong for law officers to enter a man's home without a warrant and kill both him and his son. At that time, Kernersville was a small, close-knit community where many of the residents were related or at least knew one another as friends or neighbors. It also seems that Bob Jordan was well liked by most citizens. In his interview with Pete Nash, George P. Winfree asserted that "Bob Jordan was a friend to everyone [and] would sell a farmer a horse without any down payment and would give him plenty of time to pay the bill [and if] he could not that too would be o.k." Winfree reported a number of things Bob Jordan had done for residents of the town and stated that he "was for the man that was down and out and needed help. If he was your friend he would fight for you and if your enemy it would be just too bad."

According to Winfree, the Reverend J.W. Pinnix, father of lamplighter John M. Pinnix mentioned earlier, preached the funeral for the Jordans. Reverend Pinnix was one of the most highly respected men in Kernersville and was the principal of the town's first public school. Winfree described the funeral as "probably the largest ever held in Kernersville." The procession was three quarters of a mile long. The coffins were made in Kernersville by Elias Kerner Huff. The Jordans were placed in separate wagons, with Bob Jordan in the rear. Both men were buried in what is today called the Crews-Dwiggins Cemetery located on Bethel Church Road, about three miles from Kernersville.

The gravestones of the two men are inscribed as follows. For Bob Jordan: "R.A. Jordan, born July 8, 1845, died March 9, 1896, age 51 years old, 8 months. Be ye also ready for in such hour as ye think not the Son of Man cometh." On his son Banner's stone is the following: "Born August 8, 1867 and died March 9, 1896. Be ye also ready for in such hour as ye think not the Son of Man cometh."

Both Bob Jordan and his son left widows and young children behind. From the record, it is clear that Bob Jordan's wife, Minerva, was very bitter over the way the revenue officers gunned down both her husband and son, almost certainly while she and her younger children were present. Indeed, the scene must have been mortifying.

To express her outrage and help vent her feelings, Minerva Jordan inserted a card in a Kernersville newspaper called the *Silver Advocate* that was addressed to the entire public. This clearly heartfelt message read, in its entirety, as follows:

> *To the Public,—On behalf of the claims of common humanity and justice which every one should be entitled to in this land of boasted freedom, I beg to submit through the columns of* The Silver Advocate *to each and every one the facts and circumstances which culminated in rendering my home desolate and causing two vacant chairs in my family circle.*
>
> *R.A. Jordan, my husband, was 51 years old; was not a professing Christian; but was as charitable a man as could be found any where. I look upon his death as a brutal assassination, and think that rigid measures should be taken to prevent vile murderers from killing innocent men in their own homes. We had toiled together for many long years to raise our little children that they might be a pleasure to us in our declining days; but no, the bitter chalice was drained to its dregs, and heartbroken and comfortless, I am doomed to walk the remaining days of my life in grief and despair!*
>
> *My son, Banner was 28 years old—in the prime of manhood—was loyal to his friends, and notwithstanding his short comings, was an obedient and charitable son. He was "more sinned against than sinning," and was also foully killed in his bosom of his family.*
>
> *Officers assume too much authority.*
>
> *Any man or set of men who are vile and cowardly enough to brandish revolvers and curse the infants and ladies of any family and go so far as to threaten their lives, while they are weeping for their loved ones, should be severely dealt with, and if such is the case that they are at large to continue their hellish work, public opinion should take the matter in hand and deal out justice to their kind of miserable wretches, who are only lying in wait for human blood; be it law breakers or innocent and good citizens. How much longer? Such fearful outrages as this have never before been known in any civilized community, and I pray God that such things will never again transpire in the Old North State, whose hitherto unsullied banner has been trailed in the dust, and her laws rudely violated.*

The Jordan shooting also left its indelible imprint on others in the community, one of whom, it is said, was a heartbroken girl who had been in love with Banner Jordan. To express her grief, this young lady penned a poem capturing the saga, a copy of which was provided to the authors by a direct descendant of Banner Jordan.

The Death of Bob and Banner Jordan

You all know Banner Jordan,
That brave and daring man
Two revenuers captured him
By a very simple plan.

One beautiful Monday morning
In eighteen and ninety-six,
They entered his father's house,
The appointed hour fixed.

They tracked him up the stairway,
Into an attic high,
And they knew when they entered,
That some of them must die.

The ceiling gave way beneath him,
And Banner had to fall,
It was their only chance,
And they riddled him with balls.

Four bullets entered his body,
And all of them went through.
Banner then shot Davis.
It was all that he could do.

His father at the stairway
Commanded them to stop.
They drew their deadly weapons,
And shot him on the spot.

The assassin's bullet entered
That brave and noble heart.
He crossed his hands upon his breast,
And bade farewell to earth.

Can anyone ever forget that look,
That last look at his wife?
He fell defending his son,
And thus he lost his life.

They left him cold in death,
And rushed to Banner's side—
God heard their intent prayer,
And he, too, bled and died.

Ere another sun had risen,
Ere another had sunk to rest,
They were lying side by side,
In their silent graves to rest.

Certainly the entire matter was of national as well as local interest, and varying descriptions of the deadly altercation found their way into newspapers across the country. The *New York Times* of March 10, 1896, carried the following short notice:

> *At Kernersville a fight occurred this morning between Revenue Officers James Smith and Walter Davis, and Robert Jordan and his son Banner. The officers went to Jordan's house to search for "blockade" whisky. They found one keg under his woodpile. As they attempted to enter the house the father and son began firing at them. The officers also began shooting. Robert Jordan was killed and his son was fatally injured. Both officers were also wounded.*

The story also appeared in the March 17, 1896 edition of an Iowa newspaper, the *Cedar Falls Gazette*, under the banner: "Fight with Moonshiners." This item, described as "a special from Kernersville," recites that

> *Jim Smith has been after the blockaders again, and this time with disastrous and bloody effect. Two men at Kernersville lie dead, while Smith himself*

> *and another officer are badly wounded. The Jordans, moonshiners of long standing, were attacked in their home by revenue officers, and a desperate battle followed, the moon shiners continuing the fight after being riddled with bullets.*

The story even made its way into distant South Dakota, where the *Daily Huronite* of March 13, 1896, exclaimed "Fight With Moonshiners: Two of Them Dead and Two Revenue Officers Wounded." Not only that, but the Jordan episode even appeared in *Appleton's Annual Cyclopaedia and Register of Important Events of the Year 1896*, a compilation of the most important events occurring around the world in that year. Appearing under a heading entitled "Lawlessness," it read: "In a fight between revenue officers and moonshiners in Kernersville, March 8, the two moonshiners were killed and the two revenue officers wounded."

More than three years later, the incident was still being recounted, as evidenced by a story that appeared in the November 11, 1899 edition of the *Washington Bee*, a newspaper published in the nation's capital. The story was included along with several others told by Jim Redmond, who had been a gauger (a revenue customs official assigned to collect excise tax on whiskey and the like) in Statesville, North Carolina, during the time of the Jordan shootout. Apparently Redmond sold his story to several papers, and the one published in the *Washington Bee* had this rather flamboyant headline:

> *SOME ILLICIT STILL RAIDS*
> *Thrilling Facts Told by United States Revenue Officers*
> *MEN WHO ARE HUNTED*
> *Jim Redmond, a Man Who Has been Through a Baptism of Bullets*
> *Stories That Form the Material for Richest Romance—Fight in an Attic—Terrible Battle With Pistols—Where the Use of a Pistol is as Natural as That of the Hand*

Redmond is called "a splendid type of the Kentucky gentleman, tall, strong, lithe, quick to see and act and fearless" in this story. However, he seems to have left Statesville under a cloud after penning another piece for a Philadelphia newspaper running down a number of prominent people in his former post in that town. The episode, which can be read in full in the September 7, 1897 edition of the *Landmark*, had the following headline: "Revenue Officer Redmond: He Goes to Philadelphia and Publishes Slanders About the People of North Carolina." In any event, the piece in the *Washington*

Bee contained yet another version of the battle, this one clearly favoring the two government men. It also mentions that a man named "Charley Tate, a fearless man, was also to be along" on the raid on the Jordans, but he "mistook the place and did not arrive in time." The story continues:

> *In Kernersville, N.C., there was a man named Jordan, and he had a son, Banner Jordan, who was killed in the fight which followed. The elder Jordan was not suspected, but the son was. When the officers arrived they met the elder Jordan. They told him that they had come to examine the premises. He said it was agreeable to him. On the second floor they found a half dozen barrels of illicit whisky. They rolled these out on the ground and destroyed them. But the largest store was supposed to be on the third floor, which in these country houses is an attic, with the only entrance through a manhole in the ceiling and there are no steps. A man has to remove the cover of the manhole, and, if he has no ladder, must swing himself up. When the officers asked him to remove the cover he suddenly lost all his politeness. "If you want to go up there you'll have to remove the cover yourselves," he said.*
>
> *Davis took him at his word and removed it. Smith was in the room. As soon as the cover was removed Davis leaped into the opening. He had hardly got his hands up when Banner Jordan, who was concealed there, let go with a revolver and tore Davis' right arm from the fingers to the elbow. Nevertheless, Davis kept on trying to get up, and Smith had to pull him down by main force. Just then Banner Jordan tried to shift his position, and in doing so he broke through the plastering and crashed down to the floor feet foremost, and he landed shooting with pistols in both hands. Davis pulled his pistol and shot back. He put six bullets into Jordan through and through.*
>
> *Smith was busy keeping out of the range of both the contestants. At last he found an opening, and, stealing around Jordan he put the seventh bullet into him and finished him. Then he put his left arm around Davis and started with him downstairs. In his right hand was his trusty revolver. As they got down the door opened and the elder Jordan emptied a shotgun at them. The charge struck and disabled Smith's right hand in which he held his pistol. Swift as thought he whipped the weapon into his left hand, which he never removed from around his partner, and shot the elder Jordan dead, sending him to join his son. He took no aim. They didn't do it in that country. A pistol is as natural to them as their hand, and they take no more*

> *aim than they would to throw a stone, and they can kill a bird in a treetop with a throw.*
>
> *Smith knows all the ways of the 'shiners. He used to be one himself and while he was in the heyday of his lawlessness no* Deputy *from the Government ever went after him and come back. After a half dozen had been lost this way a seventh was sent to the same country.*

The Jordan shooting was the talk of the town for many years. Even today, a few of Kernersville's older citizens can recall the basic outline of the episode as passed down to them. It certainly was then, and remains today, an interesting chapter in the history of the town.

THE CARMICHAEL MURDER AND SUICIDE

Louis F. Carmichael was born on February 5, 1841, in the Moravian community of Salem in Forsyth County, North Carolina. He was the son of Richard Carmichael and Sarah Westmoreland, who were married in Stokes County on April 1, 1817. His grandfather, Duncan Carmichael, was a Revolutionary War soldier and Patriot. Richard and Sarah were also the parents of six other children. These included four daughters, Frances, Mary Magdalene, Margaret and Minerva, and two sons, Joseph F. and William Francis, or "Frank." According to the 1850 federal census, Richard was a carpenter, a trade in which his son Louis would also follow.

There is no record of Louis's activities until 1859, when he married Adelaide Priscilla McKenzie on July 24. According to census records, Louis and his new wife were residing in Kernersville by July 1860, a town about eleven miles from Salem, where he was working as a day laborer. Living in the next household was William Asbury Griffith, who had married Louis's sister Mary Magdalene on February 22, 1848. Griffith was a blacksmith and a partner with Anderson Lewis in a coach-making firm in Kernersville. About 1857, Lewis and Griffith built their plant and their homes on the Salisbury Road (now Salisbury Street). Anderson Lewis, too, was related to Louis Carmichael, having married Louis's sister Minerva on September 25, 1856. Both Lewis and Griffith were prominent men in the growing village of Kernersville, and both were active in the Methodist Church there. The fact that his two sisters had moved to Kernersville may well have been the magnet that attracted Louis as well.

Louis and his wife had three children: a son named Robert Emory, born on September 8, 1861; a daughter, Lessie May, born September 7, 1873; and a son Walter, born about 1879. Robert's birth came as the clouds of the Civil War gathered across the nation following the election, in 1860, of Abraham Lincoln as president and the secession of the seven "Cotton Kingdom" states in February 1861 to form the Confederate States of America.

While the results of the 1860 election showed that North Carolina was largely opposed to secession, momentous events already set in motion would soon change that sentiment. Shortly after taking office in March 1861, Lincoln issued an order to resupply the federal garrison holding Fort Sumter in Charleston, South Carolina. In response, Confederate troops fired on the fort on April 12, capturing it two days later. When Lincoln issued a call on April 15 for seventy-five thousand troops to be used to suppress the insurrection, North Carolina's governor refused to comply. A few weeks later, on May 20, a convention assembled in Raleigh agreed on secession and ratified the Provisional Constitution of the Confederate States of America. Military preparations soon followed. During May and June 1861, twelve infantry companies were recruited in the northern Piedmont. Two of them were formed in Forsyth County. One, the Forsyth Grays, was mustered into service in Salem on May 24, 1861, by Captain Rufus W. Wharton. On June 17, this company and two others marched off to Danville, Virginia, where they were pressed into service as the Eleventh Regiment, North Carolina Volunteers, which soon became the Twenty-first North Carolina Infantry Regiment. Later, in April 1862, Companies B (Yadkin Gray Eagles) and E (Forsyth Grays) of the Twenty-first were detached to form the First North Carolina Sharpshooters, also known as the Ninth Battalion, North Carolina Infantry.

At the outset of the Civil War, all Confederate regiments were authorized to form musical bands. Among the Twenty-first's original six members were Frank Carmichael, the chief musician, and his brother Louis. It seems likely that both acquired their musical ability while living among the Salem Moravians, who had a deep appreciation for beautiful music.

In any event, the record shows that both Louis and Frank had enlisted in the Forsyth Grays on May 24, 1861, when the company was first formed. After the creation of the Sharpshooters, the band continued with that unit as the First Battalion Band and remained in existence to the end of the war. In fact, it was in Salem on March 23, 1865, according to a notice in the *People's Press* detailing the arrival of the First Battalion there. The paper reported that "Capt. Carmichael's Brass Band, of the 1st N.C. Battalion accompanied by a select choir of Salem ladies, entertained a very large audience in the town hall, with instrumental and vocal music" in a concert given for the benefit of the Soldiers Relief Association.

Less than two weeks later, the First Battalion was back in Virginia, where the crucial battle for Petersburg was being waged. On April 2, the Union army poured through several breaches in the Confederate lines. One of the battalion's members, Nathaniel Siewers, penned a letter to his family in which he remarked that "the band and other non-combatants have left the camp." That same evening, General Robert E. Lee withdrew his troops from Petersburg and Richmond and marched them to Appomattox Court House, where the Army of Northern Virginia surrendered on April 9, effectively ending the war.

Following the conclusion of hostilities, Louis and Frank returned home to North Carolina—Frank to Salem and Louis to Kernersville. On May 15, Louis traveled from his home to Greensboro to be paroled.

There is no further record of Louis and his family following the war until he appears in the 1880 census living in Clemmonsville Township, in Forsyth County, just to the southwest of present-day Winston-Salem. When he left Kernersville, or why, is not known. His wife, "Addie," is also listed in the census, as are children Robert, Lessie and Walter, an infant. Both Louis and son Robert were working as carpenters.

Adelaide Priscilla Carmichael died on October 15, 1892. Less than a year later, Louis remarried, to Celia Ann Dwiggins, on July 27, 1893. Celia Ann had three living children of her own, all daughters. They were Zonie, born March 12, 1884; Iva, born July 1886; and Males or Malas, born June 1890. The 1900 census shows Louis, Celia Ann and her three daughters living in Kernersville, where Louis was working as a house carpenter. However, nothing more is known about his activities there until one tragic Monday, September 26, 1904.

Many of the particulars of that eventful day are detailed in various newspaper accounts, including a lengthy one that appeared the next morning in the *Winston-Salem Journal*. It carried the headline: "Double Tragedy at Kernersville." According to its content, on the morning of September 26, about 7:30 a.m., Carmichael, "apparently in a fit of insanity," murdered his wife, slashed his stepdaughter Males Dwiggins with a razor and then killed himself.

It seems that for some time discord had existed between Carmichael and his wife, and for the past three months they had been living apart, as he had been staying with his sister Mrs. Anderson Lewis. On the Saturday preceding the incident, Carmichael had returned to his home in an effort to reconcile. However, he was confronted by his wife's second daughter, Iva Dwiggins, who ordered him out of the house, telling him never to come back. Carmichael departed "in an angry mood and with a threat that he would kill Iva unless she left him alone or would kill himself remarking, by way of emphasis, that he had nothing especially to live for anyway."

On the Sunday morning following the confrontation with Carmichael, Iva went to visit her uncle, Sam Whitt, and his family who lived on the Stokesdale Road. That afternoon, Celia Carmichael sent a note to her husband telling him that if matters were up to her alone, he could return home, but Iva would not consent to it.

The content of this message angered Louis to the verge of insanity. After eating breakfast at his sister's, he went into the room of Mr. Charley Griffith, who was also staying with Mrs. Lewis, and took a razor and a .38-caliber revolver. Then Louis proceeded to his own house on the other end of town, on the corner of Railroad and Beard Streets, not far from the Southern Railway passenger depot. He found his wife at the stove preparing breakfast. What they said is not known, but it almost surely involved Iva, whom Carmichael felt had driven him from his own home. At some point, Carmichael "proceeded to vent his anger on the wife, slashing her unmercifully with the razor" that he had taken from Griffith. The *Journal* described what happened next:

> *The mother's screams attracted her youngest daughter Malas, who was lying ill in the adjoining room and she rushed into the kitchen to ascertain the cause of the disturbance. She saw her mother and Carmichael just inside the kitchen. He was hacking Mrs. Carmichael with the razor in his right hand and holding her with his left. Just as the girl Malas came in reach, Carmichael slashed at her, inflicting a wound ten inches long, slicing her right breast entirely in two.*
>
> *Carmichael then chased the wife out into the hall, through the bedroom, hacking her at every step and finally almost decapitating her. She ran through the hall, falling into the yard just beyond the steps, and expired in a few moments.*
>
> *Carmichael, realizing the seriousness of his crime, or crazed with anger, hacked himself on the neck in five different places, then placing the pistol to his head, just behind the right ear, fired four times. Two shots went crashing through the brain, one grazed the side of his head and one went aside of the mark imbedding itself in the side of the room.*

Soon, a crowd gathered around the Carmichael house. The horrified onlookers found the nearly decapitated and slashed body of Mrs. Carmichael lying in the yard. Some of those who had converged on the scene returned home to pick up guns, "as it was conceded no sane man could have perpetrated such a crime, and he was thought to be barricaded in the house." As a result, it was some time before anyone ventured to enter the house. While the crowd was still mulling what to do, the girl Males ran from the house bleeding and screaming. Finally, a salesman named Jim Walker volunteered to go inside. There, he found Carmichael "lying on the floor in a pool of blood, and apparently in a dying condition."

Some of those who had assembled carried Celia's body back into the house, and Drs. Ashworth and Linville were summoned. Upon hearing what had happened, Ashworth went immediately to the home of Mr. William F. "Billy" Winfree, where the wounded girl, Males, had been taken. (The Winfree home stood on Bodenhamer Street, just across the railroad tracks from the Carmichael home.) There, Ashworth dressed the girl's wounds. Eighteen stitches were required. Afterward, Ashworth told the *Journal* reporter on the scene that the girl's condition was serious, but he believed she would recover "unless blood poisoning set in."

Meanwhile, Dr. Linville

> *dressed the dead woman's wounds which consisted of a gash from the corner of the forehead down the side of the face, splitting the right ear entirely, four gashes in the throat, one from ear to ear and almost entirely severing the head from the body, and another from the wrist to the tip of the third finger on the left hand apparently received in trying to ward off the razor as it descended on her.*

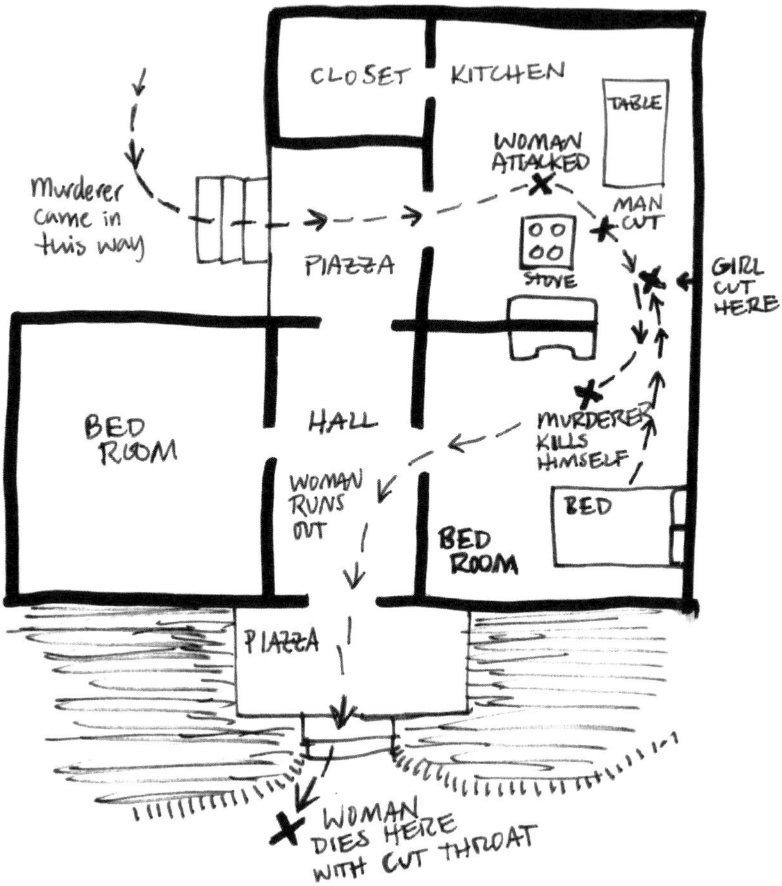

When Carmichael was lifted and placed on a bed, he was still alive, although unconscious. He did not last long, however, finally expiring about 10:30 a.m. According to the account in the *Journal*:

> *An examination of his wounds proved that the gashes in his neck would not have caused death, as only some small arteries had been severed. His wounds were bathed by Dr. Linville, and an attempt was made to locate the bullets in his head. It was found that two of them had entered the brain. As the probe was removed the brains oozed out.*

In the words of the *Journal*, prior to the tragedy Carmichael had been considered an industrious man and a good carpenter, holding a position at a box factory belonging to his brother-in-law Anderson Lewis. Celia

Dwiggins was a skilled dressmaker and "a most industrious woman," while the two daughters, Iva and Males, were employed in the Kernersville Knitting Mill on the corner of Burke and Bodenhamer Streets, not far from the Carmichael home.

Not surprisingly, other papers, both within and outside North Carolina, also picked up the story. State papers covering the tragedy included the *Landmark* of Statesville, the *Greensboro Patriot*, the *High Point Enterprise*, the *Western Sentinel* and the *Robesonian* of Lumberton. The *Washington Post* also ran a lengthy account of the tragedy on the same day that the *Journal* ran its story. All of the papers sensationalized the incident with headlines such as the one carried on September 29, 1904, in the *Western Sentinel*:

> *TRIPLE TRAGEDY AT KERNERSVILLE*
> *LOUIS CARMICHAEL, A CARPENTER, CUTS WIFE TO PIECES WITH RAZOR*
> *He Then Fatally Wounds His Wife's Daughter With a Razor, After Which He Shoots Himself, Dying in a Few Hours—Believed to Have Been Rendered Temporarily Insane—Young Girl May Recover.*

The *Greensboro Patriot* ran its version on September 28, 1904, with facts essentially identical to those in the *Journal*. It did, however, add the insight that "Carmichael was a habitual drunkard and has beaten and mistreated his wife often before and was recently jailed and fined for striking her a serious blow on the head with a stick." Undoubtedly, Louis's physical abuse of his wife contributed to the marital discord between them. Most likely, it also contributed to the ill feelings the Dwiggins children harbored toward their stepfather. The *Patriot* was kind to Celia Ann, characterizing her as "a good dutiful wife, and a Christian." It also carried the following interesting sidelight:

> *The place of the tragedy is a cottage near the station and at the time of the tragedy a crowd of Woman's Christian Temperance Union Delegates to the state convention, which met here, were waiting for the train. Some of these noble women viewed the sad spectacle of the mutilated body of the poor woman lying in her room, while the body of the poor drunkard was gasping his last in the other room.*

Ironically, Iva, the daughter who may have helped precipitate the incident, was not at home when it happened. In fact, she did not return from her uncle's house until about ten o'clock and so knew nothing of the calamity that had befallen her mother and sister until she arrived home.

The body of Celia Ann Carmichael was taken to the cemetery at Pine Grove Methodist Church, where she was laid to rest. Her husband, Louis, was interred in Kernersville in the cemetery of what is now Main Street United Methodist Church on South Main Street. The daughter Males survived the incident. She later married John Clark of Kernersville, by whom she had three daughters. No further record of Iva has been found. It has been reported that she later moved to Virginia, where she married, but this has not been proved. The oldest daughter, Zonie Dwiggins, married George P. Winfree and lived in Kernersville until her death in 1910 at the young age of twenty-six.

ADE WALKER

"A Bad Man and Dangerous Character"

Adrian W. Walker, better known as "Ade" to family and friends, was born in Kernersville on June 1, 1866. He was the son of Robert L. and Minerva Coffer Walker and a brother to John Wick Walker. Both Ade and Wick were mentioned in the story of the shootout in Kernersville involving Bob and Banner Jordan and two revenue officers. In fact, there was a close relation between the two families, as Wick's wife, Della Jordan, was Banner's sister.

Like Banner Jordan, Ade and Wick often found themselves in scrapes with the law, and drink was almost always a contributing factor. According to one story that appeared in the August 9, 1905 edition of the *Winston-Salem Journal*, Mat Richardson, "an old darkey around Kernersville," was shot by Ade Walker and "still carries the bullet in his leg." In 1900, Ade shot a man named Sidney Mitchell in front of the Salem Iron Works. While the details of the affair remain unclear, it is known that Mitchell lingered for some weeks before dying. According to a story in the April 17, 1900 *Landmark* of Statesville, North Carolina, a coroner's jury investigating the incident reached a verdict that "Mitchell came to his death through causes produced by a pistol shot." At the time, Walker was free on bond, but when Mitchell died of his wounds, Walker was arrested. Eventually, however, he successfully pleaded a case of self-defense at his trial.

It was not long, however, before Walker was once again involved with the law. This incident, which took place in 1901, began when Deputy Sheriff R.C. Hunter of Kernersville went to Ade's home to arrest him for drawing a gun and threatening to shoot a man named Foust. Refusing to surrender, Walker instead fired a shotgun at Hunter. Fortunately for the deputy, the men were at a considerable distance from each other. Even so, sixty or more shot took effect in Hunter's face, back and arm, according to a report in the *Union Republican* of Winston on September

12, 1901. And while blood flowed freely from Hunter's wounds until dressed by a physician who had arrived at the scene, his injuries were not considered life-threatening, and he walked home under his own power, albeit in great pain.

Following the shooting, Sheriff Alspaugh of Forsyth County was notified by telephone of what had happened, and he and the county jailer, a man named Thompson, took the 10:30 a.m. train to Kernersville with the aim of apprehending Walker. They returned to Winston at 3:15 p.m. with the fugitive in hand, and soon he was lodged in the county jail. According to the *Union Republican*, after shooting Hunter, Walker fled Kernersville on a bicycle, a double-barreled shotgun in his hand, and headed toward the Belew's Creek section of the county. The officers pursued on horseback, but "they had to leave their animals and track their man through fields on his bicycle." When they finally caught up with him, he was unarmed and offered no resistance. According to the paper, Walker was drunk when he shot at Hunter and "appeared to feeling the effect of strong drink when he arrived here [Winston]."

Coverage of the Hunter shooting soon found its way into other newspapers. For example, the *Times* of Richmond, Virginia, carried the story on September 11, 1901. This version styled Ade Walker as "a white man, who has the reputation of being a bad man and a dangerous character." The *Landmark* also ran a story that appeared on September 13, 1901.

Given Ade's propensity for hard drink, and considering the type of company he was accustomed to keeping, it is not surprising that he continued with his wayward behavior after the Hunter shooting. One of these incidents involved a brawl that occurred in 1903. According to the December 3, 1903 issue of the *Western Sentinel*:

> *Ade Walker and Jim Stafford of Kernersville participated in a lively scrap Saturday night. Both were drinking. Stafford hit Walker on the head with a paling, inflicting a painful wound, from which blood flowed freely for some time. He was reported to be doing well today. Walker has served a term on the county roads.*

Finally, Ade found himself in a serious incident on August 8, 1905, that ended his errant ways once and for all.

An account of what happened that fateful day appeared in the August 9, 1905 edition of the *Greensboro Patriot*. According to the story, Walker and a man named Eugene Lamar were playing cards in Granville Manuel's blacksmith shop in Kernersville. This building stood near the Southern Railway depot on what is now North Main Street, not far from its intersection with Bodenhamer Street, or the Greensboro Road as it was sometimes called. An argument began over the game, and following an exchange of words, Walker shot Lamar several times. The latter lived only a short while before succumbing to his wounds. The *Patriot* concluded its coverage of the shooting with the remark that "Walker is a well known character. He served a term on the county roads a few years ago for shooting a man." Immediately following the incident, Walker skipped from the scene.

It so happened that not five minutes after the shooting, Charles E. Ader, a member of the business staff of the *Winston-Salem Journal*, in Kernersville on other business, hurried to Manuel's blacksmith shop and began gathering details of the shooting. Ader was soon joined by a *Journal* reporter and staff artist named Fuller. Their combined efforts produced a lengthy narrative of the events of that fateful day that appeared in print on the same day as the *Greensboro Patriot* version.

According to this *Journal* report, Walker, age forty-three, shot Lamar to death in Manuel's blacksmith shop about 1:30 p.m. The paper described the scene as follows:

> *With a .38-calibre bullet hole through his right lung, and with his life's blood oozing from the wound, Lamar grappled with his assailant until Walker was unconscious. Then Lamar, whose fingers had been clutched about Walker's throat, released his vise-like grip; uttering prayers to God, calling for his old mother, and tossing in awful misery for forty minutes before he died.*

Details were also provided as to the source of the trouble, according to which it seems that on the previous day, Walker and Lamar had been gambling and Lamar had won $1.50, a sum that the paper later characterized as a "pitiful reason for the death shot." Then, shortly after dinner that same day, both men went to Manuel's smithy. Both had been drinking. Walker asked Lamar to play cards, probably hoping to recoup his loss from earlier in the day. Lamar refused, saying he would accommodate Walker at a later date. He then added, "You're drinking, and when you're drinking, you're fussy." At that, Walker replied with an oath and then blurted, "We'll shoot it out then," to which Lamar laughingly agreed.

The testimony of one witness described what happened next:

> *Walker drew his pistol and blazed away at Lamar—two bullets entering the victim, one in the right side and the other in the left leg. With the greatest nerve, although fatally wounded, Lamar pulled his gun and fired twice at Ade. Then, rushing at him, he seized Walker by the neck, thrust his gun against him, and fired three times more. One of the balls penetrated Walker's right thigh causing a painful, though not very serious wound. In the meantime, in their scuffle, they had both fallen to the ground, Lamar all the time choking and beating Walker in the face with his fist, and once reaching without success for a pick which was near his head.*

Granville Manuel was in his shop, "hammering at his anvil, just to the left of Walker and Lamar, and heard their conversation." However, after the first two shots, he headed out of the building, fearing for his life. Despite fleeing, he later stated that he was in the building long enough "to be positive that Walker shot first." Manuel hastened to find an officer of the law, but failing, he returned to his shop "only to discover Lamar in the last throes of death." According to Manuel:

> *Walker, exhausted by the struggle, had been prone upon the ground, but regained consciousness and started away from the scene. Then he turned back, swearing, "He shot me; I'm not going to run." Then he walked Cherry Street past his home and disappeared into the woods, where he was afterwards captured by Officer Flint* [sic].

Walker was given a preliminary hearing the same day before Kernersville mayor C.L. Linville and James M. Guyer, the local justice of the peace. Witnesses examined were Granville Manuel and James Perdue, both of whom gave essentially the same testimony. Walker, who was also given the opportunity to make a statement, at first refused. But later, according to the paper, "he wanted to unbosom himself, but was advised not to do so." Despite this counsel, he insisted on saying a few words. According to the *Journal*, he stated:

> *We were in Manuel's shop; I and Lamar took a drink; were feeling good; never fell out over cards; asked Lamar did he want to shoot. "Yes, I will shoot with you right now." I said, "You don't mean to shoot me, do you." Cursed and declared he did; Lamar pointed gun at me. I only shot once: Lamar tried to use* [an] *ugly pick on me.*

Following this short statement from the defendant, Mayor Linville remanded Walker to the Forsyth County jail to be held without bond.

At the time of the shooting, Lamar, born in Kernersville on September 18, 1873, was about thirty-two years old and a well digger by trade. He was married to Lucy Jane Corum and they had two young children. Eugene's mother was Lacy Ann Jordan, sister to Robert A. Jordan. She was a very religious lady and one of the ten charter members of Kernersville's First Baptist Church. According to the *Journal*, "Lamar bore a reputation of being a good-hearted fellow when sober, but rather fussy when under the influence of liquor. His courage was never questioned."

According to the paper's account, the tragedy was deepened when the "gray-haired mother of Lamar, accompanied by Mrs. Bob Jordan, whose husband and son suffered violent death at the hands of revenue officers a few years ago," arrived at Manuel's blacksmith shop. There, his mother dropped to her knees "by the side of her dying son and added her moans to his own impassioned words."

> *"Gene, 'Gene," she sobbed; "I have tried to show you the right way, but you wouldn't listen." She smoothed his heated brow, saying words that may be imagined to come from the lips of a broken-hearted mother.*
>
> *"Where is Walker?" Lamar would say, and the mother's reply come back. "Don't think of him: he is for the law. You must think of God and ask him to forgive your sins." The scene was heart-rending, but Gene Lamar died with his mother's arms about him and her words the last he heard on earth.*

A physician was called to the scene and arrived a few minutes before the end came. After Lamar died, his body was taken away on a sidecar, and he was later buried in the Crews-Dwiggins Cemetery about three miles from Kernersville. This is the same cemetery where Eugene's twin brother, James Lamar, was buried, and also where Bob and Banner Jordan were laid to rest. All four had come to violent ends.

A second story on the shooting also appeared in the August 9, 1905 edition of the *Journal*. It was reprinted in the *Western Sentinel* on August 10 and in the *Statesville Landmark* on August 11, 1905. While its basic outline followed the earlier *Journal* version, it differed in several details.

It described Walker's preliminary hearing before the Kernersville mayor and "Judge" Guyer in what the paper described as a filled courtroom. All were anxious to hear Granville Manuel, described as "the only eye witness to the shooting." No mention was made of James Perdue. According to Manuel's testimony:

> *Walker and Lamar came into his shop shortly after 1 o'clock and began discussing a game of cards which they had played that morning. The witness gathered from the conversation that Lamar had won $1.10 from Walker. The latter suggested that they play another game. "You are too drunk to play, besides you are fussy when drinking," replied Lamar, who suggested to Walker that he sober up.*
>
> *"Let's shoot it out then!" exclaimed Walker.*
>
> *"All right," answered Lamar, who was smiling, and Mr. Manuel was persuaded to believe that Eugene took Walker's remark about "shooting it out" as a joke. However, Walker pulled his pistol, an Ivery Johnson .38 caliber, and began firing upon Lamar. He shot twice in succession. Lamar then drew a .32 caliber pistol and fired, it is claimed three or more times. Lamar then went at Walker and the two men clinched. Lamar put his left*

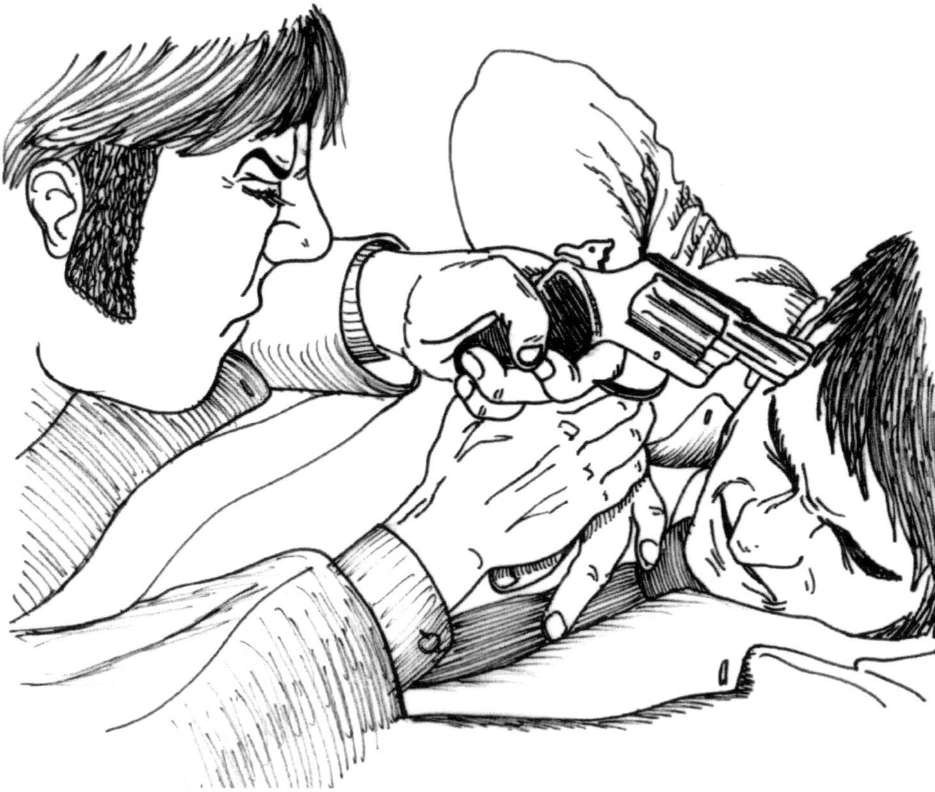

arm around Walker's neck and pressed him to the ground. At this juncture the owner of the shop fled.

"Why did you leave?" asked the court.

"Because one of those pistols was being pointed toward me," replied Manuel, who stated that he went in search of an officer, but failed to find one. Witness stated also that when he left Lamar was on top of Walker choking him.

"When I returned to the shop," continued the witness, "Walker was leaving and he was walking quite fast. I found Lamar down on his all fours. He was groaning pitifully. He died in about forty minutes after the shooting."

After Manuel was finished, Walker asked to make a statement but was advised "to say nothing until the trial in the superior court." The prisoner did, however, say that "he and Lamar had been drinking and that they had been playing cards at the brick yard every day at the noon hour." Walker also claimed "that by his remark to 'shoot it out' was meant that they shoot at a target." Though he admitted that he and Lamar had been drinking, he "denied that they fell out over a game of cards." Finally, he asserted, "It was Lamar who talked about shooting first and I asked him if he meant to shoot me and he replied that he did."

Then, in response to questions put to him by the defendant, Manuel "stated that when he left Lamar had Walker by the throat and was reaching for a big pick."

According to this version of events, "Walker has one painful wound in the left leg just above the knee, inflicted by one of the shots fired by Lamar. The ball went through the leg and the wound was dressed by a physician before the trial."

It was also stated that Walker went directly to his home after the shooting, which was located about a half mile from Kernersville, where he claimed that he decided to surrender to the authorities:

> *"I decided to go back to town and surrender," continued the defendant. "I had started when I saw John Joyce and Frank Flynt coming after me. They called upon me to surrender and I told them I had already decided to surrender. I went on with them." Walker exhibited a hole in his coat made, as he claimed, by one of the shots fired at him by Lamar. He also stated that another ball grazed his right ankle.*

It was also reported that while Walker was sitting in the train station at Kernersville, waiting for the train that would take him to jail in Winston, two small girls, who evidently knew Walker, sat down near him and questioned him about his injuries. They asked, "Ade, don't you wish you had let that whiskey alone," to which Walker replied, "Yes, I do."

Additional information was also provided in this story on both Walker and Lamar, both of whom, it was said, "were recognized in Kernersville as dangerous men when drinking." Lamar had been indicted several times for retailing bootleg whiskey. It was also reported that a few years earlier, Lamar had sustained an injury while working in a well belonging to a furniture factory in Winston. As a result, he filed suit against the company and eventually obtained a $500 judgment.

As for Walker, the *Journal* reprised several of his past misdeeds, including the shootings of Mat Richardson, Sidney Mitchell and Sheriff R.C. Hunter of Kernersville. In this version of the shooting of Hunter, Ade was said to have pulled a shotgun on Hunter, saying, "I'm not going with you and you had better go on back—move fast too." Hunter turned and was about a hundred yards or more away when he turned to look back. When he did, Walker peppered him with buckshot. At the trial, Walker claimed he had just shot for fun and did not intend to hit the deputy.

The Walker-Lamar shooting was considered big news, and coverage of the affair made its way into papers such as the *Washington Post*, which carried a story on August 9, 1905, under the banner: "Killed in Drunken Fight: Fatal Shooting Followed Accusation of Unfairness at Cards."

After several weeks in the county jail, Walker was finally tried in October. According to two stories in the *Washington Post*, both dated October 13, 1905, Walker pleaded guilty to second-degree murder for shooting Lamar. Following his plea, several character witnesses were examined, and then Walker himself asked to address the court. He "pleaded for the mercy of the court, saying that his father died when he was young, and that early in life he fell in with bad associates and began drinking," which influences, he said, were responsible for his present trouble.

After Walker was done, Judge Bryan, who was in charge of trying the case, sentenced Walker to the North Carolina state penitentiary for twenty years. The *Landmark* of Statesville ran a story on the trial on October 17, 1905. After reporting on the sentence, the paper commented, "He deserved the sentence."

While awaiting transportation to the prison at Raleigh, Walker is said to have remarked that he did not propose to let the sentence worry him. Whether it did is not known. It is known, however, that he did not serve out his entire twenty-year sentence; instead, he fell ill with a terminal illness while still in prison. He was eventually sent back to Kernersville to live out his few remaining days. He died on September 8, 1910, and his body was interred in the Mount Gur Cemetery there.

STRAY CURS WITH FANCY PEDIGREES

Samuel L. Jordan was born in Kernersville on April 16, 1878. He was the son of Robert A. "Bob" Jordan and Minerva Ballard and a younger brother to George Banner Jordan. An earlier story discussed the shootout in Kernersville in March 1896 in which Bob and Banner Jordan were killed by two revenue officers from Greensboro. That incident left Sam, eighteen years old, as the only male in the Jordan family, burdening him with the considerable responsibility of helping support his mother and unmarried sisters.

Four years later, Sam was still residing with his mother and two sisters, Elisa and Hattie, and making what money he could by operating a dog kennel. In fact, it was Sam's dog business, operated under the rather pretentious name Dan River Kennel Club, that ultimately led the young man to transgress the law.

For a while, Sam operated his establishment on the up and up, raising well-pedigreed hunting dogs and advertizing them across the country in various sporting magazines. As orders came in, he shipped the dogs out by rail to eagerly waiting customers, most of whom were well-to-do—they had to be in order to afford the prices charged.

At some point, Sam's business became so brisk that he needed help, so he took on another Kernersville lad, Elzie Linville, to assist him. Elzie, born about 1882, was the son of William A. Linville and Emma Bodenhamer. W.A. Linville was in partnership with Bob Jordan in the livery stable business a few years before Jordan was killed.

Eventually, Sam's business became too good because more orders poured in for his dogs than he could legitimately fill. Instead of nixing the extra business, Sam began to meet rising demand by shipping about any old kind of dog he could lay his hands on around town. Naturally, the customers who ended up with such dogs assumed a mistake had been made and shipped the

animals back to Sam with a request for a refund, which he conveniently ignored.

In due course, some of those who had lost money contacted the U.S. Postal Service and an inspector was assigned to investigate. The man chosen for the task was T.M. Reddy of the North Carolina district. It didn't take Reddy long to figure out the swindle Sam was working, and an arrest was made.

The news about Sam's run-in with the law reached the public on February 22, 1905, when the *Greensboro Patriot* ran a story headlined: "Dealer in Dogs Charged With Fraudulent Use of the Mails." The article informed its readers that Jordan had been given a hearing in Greensboro that day before United States commissioner Beckerdite on the charge of the fraudulent use of the mails. Bond was set at $1,000, a sum that Sam was able to meet, perhaps reflecting just how prosperous his canine venture had been. In support of the charge, Reddy had offered in evidence "a large number of letters from parties in different parts of the country who had purchased dogs of Jordan." Not only that, but "from the correspondence it was shown that each dog had the same pedigree, the same being printed on a blank form." Since it appears that Sam was in no position to rebut the charges, he kept quiet during the proceeding. The *Landmark* in Statesville also carried the news about Sam's trouble in its February 24 edition. The story was spreading fast.

On March 1, 1905, the *Patriot* of Greensboro announced that Sam's sidekick, Elzie Linville, had also appeared before Commissioner Beckerdite for "aiding and abetting Sam Jordan of Kernersville, in selling dogs." According to the story, "Linville gave $250 bond for his appearance at the next term of the Federal court at Greensboro." The story noted that "one dog was offered as evidence against the defendant, and it was said that the animal had been shipped to several states and returned, because it did not fill the recommendations made by the salesman."

Before long, other papers began to pick up the Jordan narrative, adding details—some quite colorful—about the case. For example, the *Western*

Sentinel of March 30, 1905, noted that a district attorney from Forsyth County named Holton had traveled to Greensboro to appear in the case of the Jordan dog caper. According to the paper, Sam was charged with fraudulently using the mails "in selling dogs of all sorts of high pedigrees at big prices, the fraud alleged to consist in his getting the price of a high class dog, and shipping any kind of a common dog instead." According to the *Greensboro Telegram*, "A great many witnesses will be present in this case, from all parts of the United States, to testify in behalf of the government." One of those slated to appear was "a big magnate of the Standard Oil Company in Philadelphia," who supposedly forked over $100 for a St. Bernard with a distinguished ancestral line but instead received what was described as "an Oak Ridge yellow hound." A prominent member of a wealthy New York sporting club was also summoned as a witness.

One of the more amusing headlines that appeared in connection with the Jordan story came from the *Landmark* of March 31, which proclaimed: "Dogs to Be Introduced as Witnesses in the Federal Court."

Citing the *Greensboro Telegram* as its source, the paper noted that Jordan had described highly pedigreed dogs in circulars that he sent through the mail and then defrauded purchasers who responded. According to the story, "Several of the dogs received by the purchasers on the strength of representations in these circulars will be brought here by the witnesses so that the jury can see whether they fit the description in the circulars or not." One of the buyers, the previously mentioned Standard Oil tycoon, was expected to bring with him "a common brindle-colored benched legged country-bred stump-tailed bull fice, which he thought was a hundred dollar St. Bernard until he got him."

By April 6, the story had made its way into papers outside North Carolina, including the *Washington Post*, which announced that a man from that city had been the victim of a North Carolinian who sold worthless curs as pedigreed dogs. The gentleman was characterized as "a high official at Washington," while another victim was purported to be a railroad official at Richmond. In fact the story said Postal Inspector Reddy had "traced thirty persons who had been imposed on."

On April 7, the *Landmark* ran a brief notice stating that Linville had pleaded guilty in federal court at Greensboro to charges of mail fraud and had been fined $250, which he paid. Perhaps one of the best accounts of the mess Sam and Elzie had gotten themselves into appeared in the *Landmark* on April 11, 1905, and is repeated here in its entirety. Of special note are the words of the learned judge who heard the case:

The Landmark *has been interested in the case of Mr. Jordan, of Kernersville, who advertised high pedigreed dogs and then filled the orders with any common curs he could pick up. Jordan was indicted for using the mails to defraud and plead guilty in the Federal Court at Greensboro last week. Judge Boyd first sentenced him to pay a fine of $200 and to serve 30 days in jail. At the urgent solicitation of counsel the jail sentence was remitted and the fine increased to $250. In his remarks on the case Judge Boyd said that from all appearances Jordan was engaged in sending worthless dogs out of the State, which was, in a sense, a commendable act, but he was grossly wrong in taking money for a sorry cur, under fraudulent representations; and that he could not see how anybody could want to pay $60 for a dog, stating that he was no expert on dogs, only knowing Newfoundlands, mastiffs, pointers and those box-faced things women ride in carriages with.*

Post Office Inspector Reddy, being examined by the district attorney, related how he had investigated the case. He found that Jordan, under the name of the Dan River Kennel Company, had advertised highly pedigreed dogs all over the country and received orders through the mails for many dogs, costing from $30 to $60 each; that in almost every instance the dog was returned, but no money was refunded. As soon as Jordan got the dog back he would fill another order with him. The big dog in the case—which the inspector had kept for exhibition to the jury should the case come to trial—had been reshipped seven times to parties in Nebraska, New York, Pennsylvania and South Carolina. This dog, he said, was advertised with the following pedigree: "Rushaway Rap out of Reuse of Heathecote; close relation to Lad of Rush, Jingo, Rip Rap and King of Kent." He said the dog was a stray cur about the freight yards in Winston, and last December followed a railroad man named Longworth to Kernersville. There he took up with a negro, who sold him to Jordan for $3. This dog was first shipped to Dr. A.L. Ott, a dentist of Ridgeway, S.C., December 20th; was returned by him, and the same dog had been shipped to Georgia, Pennsylvania, New York and Nebraska to prominent sportsmen, who had invariably returned him, with the statement that some mistake must have been made. He brought all the way from $30 to $50 each time, but there was never any change in his pedigree. The inspector said he had been able to establish at least thirty cases of worthless dogs being shipped, but none of them were as well traveled as the one under special consideration.

Judge Adams, in pleading for the young man, said he had had but little chance in life; that he had the support of a mother and sister on his hands, his

father and brother having been shot down in their own home in Kernersville when he was a little boy by revenue officers and killed; that he really dealt in high pedigreed dogs, but as numerous orders came in for them and the real dogs gave out, the young fellow could not resist the temptation to fill an order with any sort of dog that came handy. Judge Boyd, in remitting the imprisonment, said that as he had fined another Forsyth man at Statesville court $250 for selling pint bottles of whiskey and getting money for quart bottles, he would impose the same fine on the man who sold bench-legged fices as having descended from Rushaway Rap, Rip Rap, King of Kent and other honorable ancestors in dogdom.

The *Greensboro Patriot* of April 12 also carried a report of a brief court proceeding in which Sam entered a guilty plea:

In the Federal court last Wednesday, Samuel L. Jordan, of Kernersville, indicted for fraudulent use of the mails, through his attorneys, G.S. Hasten *and Judge S.B. Adams, pleaded guilty and Judge Boyd fined him $250. The lawyers made a strong plea for the young man, showing petitions for clemency from nearly every citizen of Kernersville. His aged mother sat at his side. Judge Boyd first fined him $200 and sentenced him to thirty days in jail, finally remitting the jail sentence and adding $50 to the fine.*

The story about Sam Jordan did not completely die even after the case officially concluded in 1905. It turns out that some years later, T.M. Reddy, the man who first apprehended Sam, spoke to a reporter at the *Washington Post* about his many adventures as a postal inspector, and the story appeared in the February 25, 1912 edition of that paper.

By that time, Reddy had been a postal inspector for twenty-two years, including several years attached to the New York office following his stint in North Carolina. He had no doubt seen many scams committed via mail fraud, and the fact that the one involving two young Kernersville boys struck him as memorable seems worth noting. This is the tale Reddy wove:

I'll tell you of an amusing case in which a number of wealthy New York sportsmen were swindled by a slick country man living at Kernersville, a little town between Greensboro and Winston Salem. Jordon [sic] *was his name—Sam Jordon—and he cleaned up $2,500 before I got him. He inserted advertisements in all the sporting journals describing his fine kennels of hunting dogs. These he offered at prices from $75 to $200. All were registered, his advertisements stated and each had a pedigree dating back a century.*

From the number of complaints that began to pour in on me, it was evident that Sam had been doing a land office business. Many of the complainants wrote that after sending their check for the dog they specified either a gun shy measly, half-breed pointer or setter would arrive, or else a letter would come from Jordon saying that the dog purchased died on the day of shipment, but as he was the property of the purchaser from the moment the check was sent the loss was his and not the writer's.

I learned that there had been an epidemic of dog stealing in and around Kernersville, but strange to say, Jordon was not suspected. Some of the dogs stolen were valuable hunting dogs but more often they were half-breeds that hung around livers stables. I soon got on Sam's trail and arrested him. He made a clean breast of the whole swindle, and he left Kernersville for the Greensboro Jail, where he served out his term. But before he was caught up

> *with, some of Kernersville's best known stray dogs were gracing the kennels of some of our wealthiest sportsmen. I might add that the same pedigree did service for every dog shipped.*

It may also be of interest to note that Reddy's story made its way into other newspapers around the country, including the *Anaconda Standard*, published in faraway Anaconda, Montana.

Not long after the dog swindle case concluded, it seems Sam left Kernersville and moved to Swan Quarter, a small town in Hyde County in the eastern part of the state. He married Clara Sawyer and together they had several children. He passed away on April 22, 1942. In the 1910 census for Swan Quarter, Sam's occupation is listed as salesman in a drugstore, so it seems he had washed his hands of the dog business and settled down to a more mundane but respectable occupation.

Unfortunately, Sam's partner, Elzie Linville, managed to get himself into the headlines one more time before finally straightening out. The news story in question appeared on December 6, 1907, in the *Western Sentinel* and involved two of Linville's other Kernersville associates, Wick Walker and George Winfree.

According to the story, Wick, "a former well-known baseball pitcher," had gone on a rampage the previous Monday with Elzie and George while all three were badly intoxicated. It seems that the threesome drove a few miles out into the country with a shotgun, presumably to do a little hunting. But since hard drink and birdshot make a poor mix, the game that was bagged on this particular expedition turned out to be Wick.

When he was brought home, his condition was regarded as critical, and there was worry that he might not make it. He was "badly swollen as a result of the large number of shot that entered his arms and body." The worst wound, and doubtless most painful, was in or near his groin, and Dr. Carlton, the Kernersville physician called to treat him, guessed "that the muzzle must have been near Walker's body when it was fired." After looking him over, Carlton decided he would leave the shot where they were, "saying they were too deep to interfere with."

Surprisingly, Wick, who was conscious after the shooting, said "he had no idea who shot him or when and how it occurred." Nor did Winfree or Linville know what happened. Both men admitted that they had been drinking but stated "that if they shot Walker they have no recollection of it." Both expressed their regret over the sad affair. Incidentally, Wick did recover and lived another fourteen years before passing away in May 1921.

Like Sam Jordan, Elzie Linville, too, moved away from Kernersville, settling in the nearby town of High Point, where by 1910 he was married and working as a laborer in a furniture factory there. He and his wife, Mary Willis, had two sons. The oldest, Frank Earl Linville, was born on June 22, 1908. The youngest, Wilborn D. Linville, died on July 16, 1918, when he was but nine months old. Elzie died sometime before January 29, 1920.

A MYSTERIOUS EXPLOSION AT THE TOWN HALL

The year 1906 proved an inauspicious one for Kernersville. First, the town's firehouse, with all its attendant equipment, burned in January. It seems that the fire was caused by the ignition of fuel stored at the firehouse and used in the town's oil-burning streetlamps. Then, in March, the town's only public school building burned to the ground, necessitating its closure.

It appears that both these incidents were accidental and unconnected. Still, they disturbed the citizens, many of whom had become disenchanted with town officials, including the mayor and the local constabulary, policeman W.R. Samuels. At the time, Samuels was the only law enforcement officer in Kernersville.

The unrest became almost palpable as warm weather approached, and tensions were heightened by the indictment of Samuels on what was termed "a serious charge"—the alleged larceny of a calf from Dr. Elias Kerner some eighteen months before.

According to a story in the June 14, 1906 edition of the *Western Sentinel*, a warrant was sworn out by Kerner, and "Samuels was cited to trial before Justice of the Peace J.M. Guyer." The hearing, the paper reported, "opened at 6:30 last evening and was concluded in an hour when the magistrate dismissed the case, taxing Dr. Kerner, the prosecutor, with the costs." Samuels was defended by Mr. Lindsay Patterson, and Mr. F.T. Baldwin appeared for the prosecution.

Several witnesses were called. Those for Samuels testified that they had been present when he purchased the calf from Kerner, agreeing to pay three dollars. On the other hand, Kerner swore that Samuels had never paid for the calf and instead had simply removed it from his pasture. In the back-and-forth that ensued, Samuels "held that Dr. Kerner owed him at the time the deal for the calf was made and he applied the $3 to the debt. On the other hand Dr. Kerner alleged that the policeman owed him." Finally, at

the close of the speeches, "Justice Guyer immediately rendered his decision acquitting the officer."

A warm summer in town became even hotter a few weeks later when the *Western Sentinel* of July 12, 1906, reported that the Kernersville mayor's office and calaboose had been dynamited on the previous Sunday morning. The paper described the event as follows:

> *The mayor's office and the "calaboose" of Kernersville, which occupy the same building, are very much in need of repairs, for along about two o'clock Sunday morning some party or parties unknown to the writer at least proceeded to put a piece of dynamite in the building and lighted the fuse. What happened when the fire reached the dynamite may easily be imagined.*
>
> *A* Sentinel *man visited Kernersville this morning—visited this enterprising little city while her citizens were yet in the land of Nod. One walking her shady, quiet streets at 6 o'clock this morning could not help*

wondering why it was that some Russian bomb-thrower should choose this pretty little town as the scene for such a deed as that committed on the previous morning. But, perhaps, 'twas not one of the Czar's subjects who was the author of this act, which, according to one man, destroyed all the property the town owns.

Be that as it may, some one put a stick of dynamite in the municipal building of Kernersville, and what that dynamite did for that building was apparent.

And—perhaps—underneath this Sunday morning tragedy there lies a story—a story of sweet revenge, a story of disapproval of certain men and certain things that be, a story that has not yet been completed!

Who can fathom the heart of a resident of Kernersville, or who there be who can foretell what will happen on the morrow in that municipality? Are not some of them "always at war, never at peace" as Judge Bynum once upon a time said of certain people.

The story continued with the report of the *Sentinel* man who went to Kernersville to investigate. According to the account in the newspaper:

He went, he saw and—he came back, and all that he can swear to is that somebody put some dynamite in the building and when the dynamite exploded the window panes shattered, the swinging lamp fell to the floor, the benches all fell to pieces, the ceiling was lifted upward and the floor went downward, a hole was torn in the side of the building, the water bucket turned over and the ink stand disappeared. We will add to this our belief that the perpetrator of this act must have smiled as he viewed the completeness of his job on the following morning.

One man told us that the motive of the whole affair was revenge. Another said that it showed that the people of the town were dissatisfied with the manner in which they are being governed; another assured us that the feeling against the policeman was "the cause of it," while Landlord Willis of the hostelry of that name says that all the "other town property has burned up and as there was a mortgage on the calaboose some of the boys thought that they would blow the mortgage off the building so that the town could have one thing it could call its own."

It seems the reporter dispatched to the scene also heard two rumors while interviewing the local citizens. One was that "Policeman Samuels would resign today and that peace would once again hover over Kernersville." The other was that "a warrant would be sworn out against Policeman Samuels, on a charge growing out of some recent matters prior to the dynamiting of the building by some one."

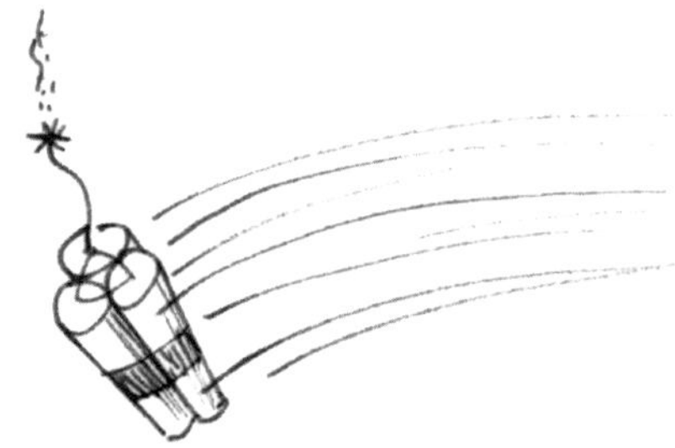

In an effort to pin down the facts, the reporter hunted down officer Samuels and asked him point blank if he intended to resign. "No Sir, I'm not going to resign," was the officer's reply. "I never had the least idea of doing such a thing." Samuels did, however, intimate that "he was being persecuted" but added that "the Lord is stronger than the devil" and that he (Samuels) "would finally make Kernersville the most peaceable spot on God's green earth."

As for the second rumor, the reporter was assured by a "prominent Kernersville man" that "before nightfall Policeman Samuels will be the defendant in a case." In any event, it seems that Samuels did not resign, as had been conjectured, nor was he indicted. Clearly, there were undercurrents in the town that the reporter was unable to discern, yet they were real and seemed to run deep.

In his final say on the incident, the *Sentinel* correspondent added that

> *there were no prisoners in the lockup Saturday night. No one was hurt, but the one time municipal building of Kernersville is in a pretty shaky condition, while every other man you meet in Kernersville looks upon the whole affair as a great big old joke—what does a Kernersville man care for expenses anyway? But taking the matter seriously, as some are, this dynamiting business is liable to put stripes on somebody—provided he is caught—and if the man who threw that dynamite keeps his mouth shut he's not very liable to be caught.*

By July 13, 1906, the story of the unrest in Kernersville had reached Statesville, where the *Landmark* reported on the dynamiting of the town's municipal building. In this account, the building was entirely wrecked, the sides blown out and the contents demolished. In addition, nearby buildings were damaged and the occupants of the Willis hotel "badly scared by the explosion." A further fact was also disclosed—on the same Saturday night the explosion occurred, the mayor was holding court in the town hall.

And while Mayor Linville's court was in session, "a stick of dynamite was exploded about 200 feet from the city hall giving the entire neighborhood a heavy jar, and it is supposed that the same parties blew up the hall later on in the night."

Matters grew "curiouser and curiouser" a few days after the explosive blast at town hall when, according to the *Western Sentinel* of July 19, 1906, Mayor Linville sent a telegram asking Deputy Sheriff Hutchins to bring bloodhounds to the Kernersville Town Hall on the 10:50 train. No explanation was given, and the paper reported that "parties coming in from Kernersville this afternoon said they had not heard of any trouble." The report did confirm that "since the blowing up of the mayor's office and calaboose by dynamite there has been much discussion between the two factions which have existed for some time." It seemed that one group wanted the mayor and chief of police to resign, and according to a report by one of the town's citizens, "there have been several small dynamite explosions since the mayor's office and calaboose were wrecked and the opinion was expressed here this afternoon that Mayor Linville had a clue to the guilty parties and wanted the bloodhounds to aid him in capturing them." However, fearing for the safety of his canine friends, Deputy Hutchins wanted "a guarantee that he and his dogs will not be blown up before he enters the gates of that town." Evidently no such assurance was forthcoming and the dogs were a no-show.

Less than a week after the mayor's plea for bloodhounds, another peculiar event occurred. This was reported in the July 26, 1906 *Western Sentinel.* It seems that a few days before, "a pistol was found about a mile down the railroad track about a half mile from Kernersville and it was currently reported that it belonged to Mr. Jess Bowers, a young man working at the Kernersville Furniture Co." Policeman Samuels was dispatched to the boardinghouse where the young man resided, and the officer found him sick in bed. Undeterred, Samuels "demanded that Bowers get up and go up town with him and Bowers asked him what for," to which Samuels replied, "I will tell you when we get up town." Bowers refused and ordered the officer out

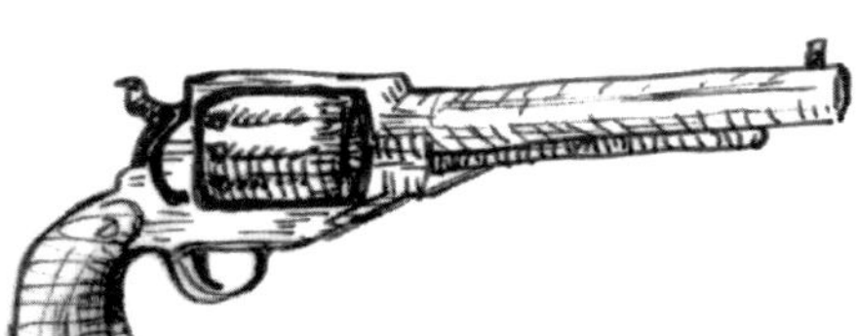

of the house, locking the door on him. The next day, however, Samuels returned with a warrant, and Bowers's trial "came off Saturday night at 7 o'clock in the mayor's office, which was recently almost totally destroyed by an explosion of dynamite." This inquiry must have been of considerable interest to the town's citizens because the report in the paper noted that some two hundred people were present.

During the hearing, Mayor Linville "sprang a surprise by asking questions tending to show that the defendant had been 'turning loose' the dynamite." Mr. G.H. Hasten, counsel for the defense, strongly objected, pointing out that the mayor was addressing a charge not contained in the warrant. The objection was sustained and the assertion stricken from the record. Moreover, when Hasten had his turn to address the court, "he bitterly denounced Samuels for his interference, and at the mention of Samuels' name the spectators hooted and jeered the officer."

In the face of this outburst, the mayor "ordered the whole 'bunch' under arrest, but later declared that he did not know a single person who raised the disturbance but said that if it could be proved on them that he would send them to jail." Fearing that he, too, would be thrown into the hoosegow, "one little boy over in the corner on hearing the mayor's order for arrest declared, 'I never said a word.'"

According to the report in the *Western Sentinel*, several witnesses were examined, but no proof was ever adduced to show that the "pistol would shoot or that it belonged to young Bowers." Stymied but not deterred, the mayor declared that he would reserve "his decision until he could make further investigation as to whether the pistol would shoot or not."

The trial of young Bowers lasted until rather late at night, and "while the mayor was sitting on the case some one was robbing his store." In fact, about $500 worth of jewelry and merchandise was pilfered. The theft, however, was not detected until early the following morning, at which time bloodhounds were brought to Kernersville to track down the thieves. However, the dogs arrived too late to be of help, as crowds had already trampled over the trail of the perpetrators.

It seems, however, that "there were evidences that the robbers had gone toward Greensboro and about 500 people on horseback and in buggies went down the railroad about five miles but returned without any clue as to the guilty parties."

Things must have eventually settled down, as no further reports of dynamiting seem to have emerged. What all the ruckus was about is still a mystery, and will likely remain so, as all those who could shed light on the matter have long since departed for, hopefully, a more serene place.

THE GREAT BANK ROBBERY

During the first decade of the nineteenth century, Kernersville established its two earliest banking institutions. The first to open its doors was the Bank of Kernersville. Established in January 1903 by Walter Hill Mendenhall and W.S. Linville, the bank was housed in a two-story brick building that occupied the southwest corner of Main and Mountain Streets in the center of town.

The second, called Forsyth Bank and Trust Company, opened for business in 1906. J. Van Lindley of Pomona, a community near Greensboro, was its president and James M. Guyer was cashier. Guyer had been for some years a prominent civic leader and citizen of Kernersville and longtime justice of the peace. He was known locally as "Judge Guyer." He resided in a two-story frame house on the west side of North Main Street, and the bank was housed in a building on the other side of North Main, a short distance away.

By all indications, both banks prospered in the growing town and business was carried on in an uneventful manner—until one day in February 1909, when the latter institution was robbed by one of the town's own citizens.

The perpetrator was a quiet, solitary young fellow named Gaither Columbus Bodenhamer. Born August 12, 1882, he was the son of Jacob Franklin "Mr. Jake" Bodenhamer and his first wife, Elvira Core. Mr. Jake, a well-liked citizen of Kernersville, operated a small general store not far from the old W.C. Stafford store on North Main Street.

According to a statement by D.W. Harmon, vice-president and assistant cashier of Forsyth Bank and Trust, and carried in the February 26, 1909 edition of the *Winston-Salem Journal*, the theft was committed just after noon on Monday, February 8.

It seems that Guyer went to dinner (a meal called lunch by many today) and left the vault open, which appears to have been his usual practice and was not considered especially odd, since the bank was located on the busiest street in town.

As it happened, Bodenhamer was watching all of this transpire and, as the *Journal* article put it, "as soon as the Cashier was safely out of the way, the young man forced the front door open, took the money from the vault and walked quietly out of the bank." On February 10, two days later, Bodenhamer boarded a train and departed for points north, including New York City and Washington, D.C.

The first newspaper to break the story of the larcenous caper in Kernersville was the February 24, 1909 edition of the *Washington Post*, which carried the story under the headline: "Accused of Bank Robbery, Man from Tarheel Town Arrested on Charge of Stealing $2,500." The *Post* reported that Bodenhamer, then twenty-six, was taken into custody by Pinkerton detectives in Washington, D.C., at the National Hotel "on information furnished by a private detective agency of Baltimore." Bodenhamer was held at the First Precinct Police Station in Washington pending the arrival of North Carolina authorities with extradition papers.

Other newspapers soon followed up on the story, adding additional particulars. For example, the February 25, 1909 edition of the *New York Tribune* reported that a jar of gold coins totaling $1,225, allegedly "part of the money taken from the vaults of the *Forsyth Bank and Trust Company* of Kernersville, N.C., was dug up today from beneath the dwelling house in that city, where it had been buried by the robber, according to advices received here tonight." The paper further noted that Deputy Sheriff Robert Flynt of Kernersville had left Washington for North Carolina with young Bodenhamer in tow.

The following day, February 25, 1909, the *Winston-Salem Journal* carried news of Bodenhamer's arrest in Washington, D.C. The paper added that Bodenhamer had "made a written confession of the crime and when the news of the arrest and confession reached Kernersville the bank officials made a search and found money buried in a glass jar under the porch of his home." It was conjectured that "the young man had been closely watched by detectives and it is presumed that this caused him to be unable to remove the money from its hiding place." The story also carried a bit of welcome news for customers of the bank, which was that "the bank will lose nothing, as burglar insurance is carried, and the insurance company will be required to pay the expense attached to the arrest and trial."

The *Journal*'s follow-up piece on February 26, 1909, informed its readers that Bodenhamer had been brought to Kernersville by Deputy Sheriff Flynt on the seven o'clock train. He was taken immediately before Kernersville mayor C.L. Linville, where he waived examination. The

mayor then ordered Bodenhamer placed under $2,000 bond, following which he was removed to Winston-Salem, where he was lodged in the county jail to await further proceedings.

The *Journal* reported that Bodenhamer left town soon after he pinched the money, but he apparently came back the following Friday (February 12) and stayed about an hour. He returned again at a later date, staying for some time before departing town again. It took bank officials several days before they actually discovered that money was missing because it was from a reserve fund that was not counted every day. Nevertheless, as soon as the theft was detected, bank officials employed a Pinkerton detective to investigate. The agent tracked Bodenhamer to Greensboro and then on to Washington. Upon capture, Bodenhamer confessed and provided authorities with information that helped them reclaim some of the stolen money. Following up on that information, officers found considerable cash in a glass jar buried under the porch of Bodenhamer's home. In addition, Bodenhamer was carrying about $200 in cash when he was apprehended and was in possession of a costly diamond ring.

Interestingly, the *Journal* article also speculated that Bodenhamer would enter a plea of insanity at trial, commenting:

> *There is little doubt but that Bodenhamer's plea will be insanity. He seemed to have a mania for stealing and a Kernersville man told the* Journal *reporter that in his opinion the young man was unquestionably insane. He is said to have lived rather a solitary life, working when he pleased, and loafing when he pleased, and wearing good clothes all the while. His sedentary life gave little opportunity for the making of friends, and people generally seemed to look upon him as "queer."*

The *Western Sentinel*, another Winston-Salem newspaper, also reported on the robbery in its February 27, 1909 edition, noting that, when Bodenhamer was arrested, he had $200 of the stolen money in his pockets and also a $425 diamond ring, "which he said he purchased from a jeweler in New York." It seems that "the jeweler has consented to take the ring back and refund the money paid for it." The paper stated that the glass jar under Bodenhamer's porch contained $1,225 instead of the initially reported sum of $2,000, and that "the balance of the stolen funds is supposed to have been spent by the defendant during his pleasure trip north." Following his confession, a detective, along with W.F. Winfree of Kernersville, visited the place designated by Bodenhamer and "secured the $1,225 which was buried in a fruit jar and returned to the bank." This paper, too, remarked that "some of Bodenhamer's friends are contending that he is mentally unbalanced and the opinion is expressed that the insanity plea will likely be brought out at the trial."

On March 2, 1909, the *Western Sentinel* continued its account, drawn from Bodenhamer's own description. While lodged in his jail cell, Bodenhamer was visited by a *Sentinel* reporter accompanied by several other individuals, including Sheriff Ziglar, Mr. T.S. Fleshman and C.M. McKaughan. The defendant, according to this account, "was found lying in a swinging hammock and when he discovered who his visitors were he threw his coat over his head and acted as though overcome with shame at his crime. Finally at the request of the newspaper man, the prisoner arose, came to one corner of the cell and answered all questions put to him."

Bodenhamer confirmed that he had stolen the money on February 8 while the cashier, J.M. Guyer, was at dinner, gaining "entrance by slipping his hand through the glass in the door and turning the night latch." The *Sentinel* correspondent then asked, "Why didn't you take all the money in sight?" Bodenhamer replied, "I did come very near it." Bodenhamer added that he could give no reason as to why he took the money. According to his statement, "he had not planned the robbery before hand, but just fell into the trap without thinking much about it."

When asked about putting the money in the fruit jar and burying it, Bodenhamer replied that he had done that on the same afternoon he took it.

Upon further inquiry, "Bodenhamer stated that he left Kernersville on February 10th, two days after the robbery and that he made two visits to New York. While in that city he purchased a diamond ring for $425 and a diamond shirt stud for $10." As reported in the *Sentinel*, both of these were "turned over to the detectives who arrested him and will be returned to the jeweler from whom they were purchased, he having consented to refund the cash received for them."

Bodenhamer also stated that he was in his hotel room in Washington when the detectives first came after him. He described his arrest as follows:

> *His door was locked and he refused to open it the first time he heard the knock on it. A few minutes later a bell boy came up and told Bodenhamer that he had a telegram for him. When the door was opened the detectives walked in and notified him that he was wanted for robbing the Kernersville bank. It was then that Bodenhamer confessed his guilt and wrote out a statement telling how he got the money, etc.*

As told by the prisoner, he didn't "think he got as much as $2,250 and that he did not spend over $250, besides the $465 [*sic*] paid for the diamond ring and shirt stud."

Following the report of this interview, the paper concluded, "It is alleged by some that Bodenhamer is a kleptomaniac and that the plea for the defendant will be insanity."

While there was considerable reporting on the robbery and Bodenhamer's arrest, a newspaper account of the trial has not yet been found. It is believed, however, that he pleaded guilty. And from other sources, it is known that he received a sentence of five years' imprisonment.

Following his release from the penitentiary in Raleigh, either in late 1914 or early 1915, it appears that Bodenhamer traveled to the Midwest, where he may have resided for a while with his half brother, Grover Clarence Bodenhamer, who was working there as a trainman for the Norfolk & Western Railroad. Clarence, or Grover as he was later more commonly known, had been living in Portsmouth, Ohio, a town on the Ohio River in the southern part of the state, but he later moved to Richmond, Indiana, leaving a portion of his earnings on deposit at the First National Bank of Portsmouth.

Somehow, Gaither learned of his half brother's bank account and decided to help himself to the funds it contained. According to an article in the May 10, 1915 edition of the *Portsmouth Daily Times*:

> *Details of a smooth forgery worked upon a local bank last March and how the big detective agencies relentlessly follow forgers, became public today, after word had been received that Gaither Bodenhamer, the alleged forger, was under arrest at Sioux Falls, South Dakota. Sheriff Smith, while in Columbus, Saturday, secured requisition papers for his return to this state, and he will be brought back here to stand trial.*
>
> *On March 4th last, a man pretending to be Clarence Bodenhamer appeared at this bank with his pass book, and made application for a portion of the savings, giving a check for the amount. After comparing the signature of the check with that on the book, the bank officials decided that he was who he claimed to be and gave him the money. Again on March 11th he presented himself at the bank and drew out the balance.*
>
> *About April 1st, the real Clarence Bodenhamer wrote from Richmond, Ind. to the bank and asked that his money be forwarded to him. The bank refused, claiming that the money had been withdrawn. He then came to Portsmouth in person, and after thoroughly establishing his identity, obtained the full amount due him.*

> *Detectives were then placed on the trail of the alleged impostor, and they suspicioned Bodenhamer's half brother, who was traced to Chicago, and then to Sioux Falls, S.D., where he was placed under arrest.*
>
> *Local authorities have since received word that he is wanted in Sioux Falls on a charge of raising a check, and he can not be returned here until his case is disposed of there. Sheriff Smith had intended leaving for him Tuesday morning.*

On August 5, 1915, the *Portsmouth Daily Times* ran a follow-up story, which reported that Sheriff Smith had departed for Sioux Falls to take Bodenhamer into custody and return him to Portsmouth to face forgery charges. By this time, Bodenhamer had completed a sentence in a South Dakota prison for check-raising and was being held there pending the arrival of Smith with extradition papers.

A subsequent edition of the paper, dated August 13, 1915, reported that Bodenhamer had been arraigned in Portsmouth before one Squire Finney on August 12, at which time he was bound over to the grand jury. According to the paper, "Sheriff Smith says that Bodenhamer admits his guilt and will throw himself on the mercy of the court."

According to a final article that appeared in the *Portsmouth Daily Times* on September 20, 1915:

> *Gaither Bodenhamer, the Indiana man arrested at Sioux Falls, N.D., on a charge of forging his brother's name to a receipt for $75 out of his brother's savings account at the First National bank last March, entered a plea of guilty to that indictment* [and] *was given an indeterminate sentence in the Ohio penitentiary.*

The story added that he was also indicted on three other charges. They included "forging his brother's name to a $25 receipt, and two indictments charging him with passing the forged receipts." The former charge was "continued off the docket," while the other two indictments were nollied on motion of prosecuting attorney Micklethwait. During his hearing, Bodenhamer "admitted to having served a five year sentence in the North Carolina penitentiary on a grand larceny charge," stemming from the bank robbery in Kernersville.

It is not known how long Bodenhamer remained in prison in Ohio. However, it is certain that he was back in Kernersville by September 19, 1924, because he was married there on that date to Eva Wilson. Perhaps his marriage finally dissuaded him from a further life of crime, or perhaps he had seen all he wanted of the inside of the "big house." In any case, he settled down and lived as a solid citizen, operating a small Shell gasoline station on the northeast corner of Bodenhamer and North Main Streets, an occupation he pursued until his death in November 1960.

YEGGMEN AND THE TOWN POST OFFICE

According to the official records of the postmaster general of the United States, the first post office in what is now Kernersville was established on October 1, 1809, while the place was still called Dobson's Cross Roads. Its postmaster was a gentleman named Thomas Adams, of whom nothing is known. This was while the crossroads property belonged to a Moravian residing in Salem named Nathaniel Shober. Since Shober himself did not move to the crossroads until 1811, it seems likely that Adams operated the inn and store there on Shober's behalf. Incidentally, Shober succeeded Adams as postmaster on March 17, 1812.

The post office called Dobson's Cross Roads was renamed Kerner's Cross Roads about 1829 while Joseph Kerner was postmaster. His son Philip succeeded him as postmaster on April 26, 1832, a position he held until 1849, when William P. Henley, who had purchased Philip's share of his father's estate, including the store and hotel on the town square, became postmaster. Henley remained postmaster until September 30, 1854. Up until this point, it seems quite likely that the post office was located in the store on the northeast corner of present-day Main and Mountain Streets, in part of what had at one time been Dobson's Tavern.

John H. Hester became postmaster on February 18, 1858. He lived on what is now South Main Street, and it may be that the post office, during his tenure, was operated out of his house, or perhaps it was located in his store in town.

No doubt the location of Kernersville's post office moved around several more times during the nineteenth century. However, by 1905, it was located on North Main Street in a building erected for that purpose by Dr. Carey C. Sapp. This was about where 112 North Main Street is located today. It remained in this block of buildings through April 1924, but by 1935, the post office had been relocated to what is today part of the Wolfe & Associates law office building but was, in 1935, Pinnix Drug Store.

During the last quarter of the nineteenth century, post offices such as the one in Kernersville increasingly became the target of robbers widely known as yeggs or yeggmen. This term originated with gypsies to describe a clever thief selected as the tribe's chief thief, or "yegg" in their parlance.

Post office robberies were most typically carried out by two or more yeggmen operating as a team. One such team struck the post office at Kernersville on the night of October 8, 1909. One account of the robbery appeared on October 8 in the *Washington Post*:

> *Kernersville, N.C., Oct. 8.—The post office here was robbed last night. The safe was opened by the use of a railroad pinch bar. The burglars failed to find about $200 in small change, but carried off stamps amounting to more than $1,500.*
>
> *The postmaster had deposited yesterday's receipts in the bank, located in an adjoining building, which was not molested.*

Another account, this one containing a few additional details, appeared in the *Greensboro Daily News* of October 9. It repeated that the building had been robbed the previous night and that its safe was cracked by a railroad pinch bar—a long steel bar with a U-shaped claw at one end and a chisel point at the other, often used as a lever for prying railroad tracks into alignment.

It was again reported that the yeggmen failed to find any money but did carry off a large quantity of postage stamps that amounted to over $1,000. Some residents who lived near the post office claimed they had heard hammering on the safe between two and three o'clock that morning. It was also reported that a traveling man, or drummer as they were often called, staying at a hotel—perhaps the old Auto Inn on a nearby corner—rose from his bed and went behind the post office, where he "saw a man hammering on the safe and heard two men talking, but gave no alarm, for the reason he was not armed."

The financial loss to the post office could have been greater had the postmaster not deposited the sales from the previous day in the bank located in an adjoining building. At the time of the robbery, the Kernersville postmaster was Branson R. Beeson, son of Hugh and Jane (Fulp) Beeson. The adjacent bank was the Forsyth Bank and Trust Company, which had opened in 1906.

The newspaper account of the robbery concluded with a note that officials were investigating the incident but that the yeggmen had left very little in the way of clues. While it is not certain, it is likely that one of the perpetrators who carried out the 1909 Kernersville post office robbery was a man called Old Bob, known to his fellows in crime as "king of the yeggs." Several pages describing his career can be found in the book by Melville Davisson Post called *The Man Hunters*.

According to Post, Old Bob spent most of his life, some fifty years at least, in jails and penitentiaries around the country on charges related to various robberies and break-ins. On April 25, 1911, he was sentenced at Salisbury, North Carolina, to three years in federal prison in Atlanta, Georgia, for burglarizing post offices at Kernersville, Walnut Cove and Mocksville, three small towns in Piedmont, North Carolina. The burglary at Kernersville was almost certainly the October 1909 heist. Post tells us that during the latter days of his career, Old Bob confined himself to post office robberies, reasoning that, should he be caught, he would typically receive a relatively short sentence. Besides, stolen stamps were almost as good as money to Old Bob, who usually disposed of them through a fence at Coney Island, New York, for about ninety cents on the dollar.

It is said that Old Bob received the appellation "king of the yeggs" because of his pioneering work in devising ways to escape incarceration. A story that appeared in a New York paper, the *Kingston Daily Freeman*, on October 3, 1917, titled "King of Yeggmen: Title Won by Old Bob as Result of Clever Tricks," elaborates. One of the more famous methods was the so-called pocket piece, a clever trick for carrying saws. As recounted by Post:

> *When the authorities at a local prison, a county jail or station house searched the prisoner they would find an old trade dollar or a worn five-franc piece in his possession. The criminal would ask the authorities to permit him to keep it because it belonged to some member of his family—his mother, his father or some imaginary child that had cut its teeth on the metal edge in some imaginary former happy home. It was a line of what the underworld calls soft stuff, and the prisoner was usually able to put it over at the county jail. He was allowed to take the coin into the cell with him; what danger could there be in a worn pocket piece treasured for its memories?*
>
> *There were all kinds of dangers in it. The faces of the coin screwed together on delicate threads, and the interior was filled with tiny saws of the best material. For a long time through this device the clever criminal was able to get about with a fair equipment of saws in his possession...It was Old Bob, we are told, who invented the system of planting saws about in the various prisons that he might again be unfortunate enough to enter. His method was clever and ingenious. Kindly religious people endeavor to*

> *reform criminals by sending tracts and literature to the local prison. The yegg inaugurated the habit of pasting these moral dissertations on the wall of the cell. The custom pleased the very well-meaning people and it could not be very well objected to by the prison authorities. It was also useful to the yeggmen!*
>
> *The little sermons were glued to the wall with sirup* [sic], *usually a staple of the prisoner's diet. A thin saw of the best quality was thereby held in place for the benefit of the yeggmen if he should ever by chance return that way, or for the benefit of any member of the gang who might happen to be picked up by the police. It was a long time before the authorities discovered this trick, and then they found the local prisons of the country to be cached with the handy burglar tool.*

Other clever tricks used by yeggmen like Old Bob included hiding small saws in the collars of shirts and jackets and in trouser cuffs and suspending them on fine threads behind radiators. There were many others as well.

Following the 1909 robbery, things remained quiet at the post office in Kernersville until 1913, when yeggs again paid the town a visit. According to the *Western Sentinel* of June 10, 1913, sometime after midnight on Saturday, June 7, the post office was blown open and "$52.08 in money and $1,239.90 in one and two cent stamps was stolen." It appears the yeggmen responsible for the crime "entered at the front door of the building by breaking the lock with a pick which had been taken from a railroad section house nearby." Upon gaining entrance, the door of the iron safe "was broken into pieces by some kind of explosive," although none of the town residents claimed to have heard the explosion. The robbery itself was not discovered until 6:15 on the following Sunday morning.

An article called "The Pinkertons" that appeared in 1905 in the *American Illustrated Magazine* discusses the history and methods of the yeggmen. They confined "themselves chiefly to the blowing up of safes, and they commonly use nitro-glycerine as an explosive." According to the author, Charles Francis Bourke:

> *Students of criminology declare that the great recent increase in the number of safe-blowing "yeggs" is largely due to the fact that the work of digging the Chicago drainage canal, and other similar engineering feats, made so many irresponsible and reckless men thoroughly familiar with and expert in the handling of dynamite, nitro-glycerine and other high explosives which are used in blasting.*

As reported in the *Western Sentinel*, following the 1913 robbery at Kernersville, Postal Inspector Hodgin of Greensboro came to town on Sunday after the break-in to investigate but secured few real clues. He did conclude that the "robbery was the work of professional yeggmen," perhaps an unsurprising deduction. The paper also reported that some people in town "heard a rumbling noise about 2 o'clock Sunday morning and it is presumed this was the explosion that blew the safe." However, it seems none of the locals was curious enough to investigate, nor did the blast arouse any constables. After the incident, Forsyth County sheriff Flynt and his deputies traveled to Kernersville, where they assisted Inspector Hodgin, but little came of the effort and it appears no arrests were made.

One final report on the June 1913 post office robbery appeared in the *Robesonian* of Lumberton, North Carolina, in the June 12 edition of the paper. This account, picked up from the *Greensboro Daily News* of June 9, had the following to say:

> *Sunday morning about the time the* Daily News *was printing the weekly story about the activities of "Yeggmen" throughout the country, a number of them were working with their tools and explosives on the safe in the United States postoffice at Kernersville, a small place 18 miles northwest of Greensboro on the Winston-Salem branch of the Southern Railway, thus providing as it were a bit of local color for the stories which have been told of yeggish activities in this section generally.*
>
> *The burglars upon blowing open the safe secured $1,263 in stamps and $50 in cash. The stamps ranged in donation from the 1's to, the 25's, the latter of which is the highest of the parcel post denomination. The theft was discovered yesterday morning at 6:30 o'clock when the postmaster went to the postoffice.*
>
> *Postoffice Inspector I.W. Hodgin, Greensboro, was notified and spent yesterday at Kernersville taking note of the situation and hunting for clues. Returning last night he said there were scanty clues as to the parties who, supposedly, had four or five hours start.*
>
> *The work was so neatly done there was no doubt they were professionals. It was thought there were three of them, they usually going on such jobs with this number.*

There is also a record of one final assault on the Kernersville post office, this one in 1922. Of the three robberies, it seems to have netted the largest proceeds.

The *Bee* of Danville, Virginia, described the robbery in its March 22, 1922 edition in a story titled "Yeggmen Busy in North Carolina." It appears that at about two o'clock on the morning of March 21, several yeggmen broke into the Kernersville post office "and by the use of nitroglycerine, blew open the two doors on the safe, from which they secured $8,000 or $9,000 in money, stamps, liberty bonds and other valuable papers."

Cashier George V. Fulp of the Bank of Kernersville reported that "$3,200 in government bonds were sent to him by registered mail yesterday afternoon by the Wachovia Bank and Trust company of this city [Winston-Salem]." In addition, another letter "contained a stock certificate for $2,200 of Bailey Bros. Inc., addressed to Mr. Fulp." A third registered letter "contained a stock certificate for the same amount from the same concern for M.V. King, of Kernersville," while "a fourth registered letter was $150 in currency." Mr. M.V. King was Kernersville resident Monja Vesper King, whose wife was Nell Davis, daughter of Kernersville businessman E. Grant Davis. The King home was adjacent to the old First Baptist Church on North Main Street.

According to the Danville paper, the only clue that the yeggmen left behind was a brown overcoat and the tools used to break into the post office that they had taken from a local blacksmith shop. Once again, postal authorities in Greensboro were notified of the robbery and an inspector came to investigate; again, it seems, with little success.

THE RIDER WHO SHOT CONDUCTOR HOLDEN

In early 1873, the Northwestern North Carolina Railroad (NNCR) came to Kernersville, connecting it with the nearby towns of Winston, Salem and Greensboro and points beyond. The arrival of the train in the tranquil village at the crossroads soon became the talk of the town, prompting the following letter to the editor that appeared in the February 13, 1873 edition of the *People's Press* in Winston:

> *Messrs Editors: The approach of the iron horse is waking up things about our formerly quiet little town. Business is more brisk, and everything is trying to go by steam. We even imagine chanticleer tries to imitate the locomotive whistle in his cock-a-doodle-do. The switch is being laid at the depot, and Dr. Mendenhall has given orders "to surface the road" to this place. A freight train will be run from Greensboro to this place as soon as everything can be arranged.*
>
> *Your correspondent has been down the road to Greensboro, and finds it smoother than the old N.N.C.R. The rails are connected with "fish-bar-places" which tie them down very solidly. In running, the road has a clear ring, and not the usual "clatter-bang." The road is considerably shortened by running by the Button Factory, at which station houses are being built.*
>
> *Mr. Harmon is pushing the depot to completion. The well is finished and the tank is under construction.*

Over the years, the NNCR went through several changes. In 1891, it gave a ninety-nine-year lease to the Richmond & Danville Railroad, but the financial panic of the early 1890s swamped that line and most others in the country. As a result, the company was reorganized by J.P. Morgan as the Southern Railway in July 1894.

After the NNCR was completed, trains began to run regularly between Winston and Greensboro. A schedule that appeared in the June 15, 1883 edition of the *Kernersville News* gives some idea of the daily schedule at that time.

> *Leave Salem daily, 5:45 a.m.*
> *Ar've Kernersville, 6:20 a.m.*
> *L've Greensboro, 10:22 a.m.*
> *Ar've Kernersville, 11:30 a.m.*
> *Evening Trains Daily, Except Sunday*
> *Leave Salem, 5:40 p.m.*
> *Ar've Kernersville, 6:20 p.m.*
> *Leave Greensboro, 10:15 p.m.*
> *Ar've Kernersville, 11:20 p.m.*

During one of the regular runs of the Southern Railway passenger train on the evening of March 22, 1912, an incident occurred that nearly resulted in a lynching.

According to the March 23, 1912 *Greensboro Daily News*, the 8:16 p.m. train pulled out of Winston headed to Kernersville and then on to Greensboro. Its conductor, Captain Edward S. Holden, was busy checking tickets. He discovered that Fuel Hairston, a Negro, did not have one. In fact, Hairston, a bellboy at the Hotel Clegg in Greensboro, had frequently boarded the train in Winston without a ticket, and because he knew Holden, "always wanted him to pass him." But Holden refused this particular evening and demanded that Hairston come up with cash to cover the fare. Hairston grudgingly paid the conductor but later became offensive, and words were passed between the two.

Eventually, the train made its regularly scheduled stop at the Kernersville depot. Hairston got off the train but, instead of walking away, stood near the steps to the platform. After a few minutes, Conductor Holden called "All aboard!" and started to climb back onto the train. At that point, "Hairston said, with an oath, 'Take that,' and two shots rang out, both taking effect in Holden: one in the thigh, the other in the leg." Sensing what had happened, Holden called to some men standing near the platform that Hairston had shot him and directed them to stop him before he could escape. However, their effort failed, and Hairston fled into the darkness.

Following the shooting, Holden was taken back aboard the train, which departed for Greensboro. Some friends bathed the gunshot wounds in hydrogen peroxide to help reduce the risk of infection. When the train arrived in Greensboro, Holden was met by Dr. E.R. Michaux of that city,

who dressed his two wounds. Fortunately, both were in the fleshy parts of his body. As stated in the paper, "Neither was considered of a serious nature and he returned to Winston-Salem at 10:30 o'clock, his train being held an hour" while the doctor attended him. "A probe for the bullets was made, but was unsuccessful."

The *Winston-Salem Journal* also reported on the shooting the same day:

> *CAPT. HOLDEN SHOT BY NEGRO*
> *Conductor Wounded as He Boards Train in Kernersville*
> *NEGRO STILL AT LARGE*
> *But Special Train Carried Officers to Scene Last Night to Make Arrest*

The *Journal* version reported that, after shooting Holden, Hairston "stood for one moment with smoking pistol in his hand and then turned and fled into the dark night and no trace of him has been found early this morning." It also further assessed the conductor's condition, noting that when the 11:25 p.m. train with Holden onboard reached Winston-Salem, many of his friends were there to meet him. "An ambulance and stretcher were in readiness at the station but the stretcher was not needed, as Captain Holden was able to take his seat calmly in the machine and proceeded to his home as if nothing had occurred." After reaching his home on Main Street, Holden was attended to by Dr. Bahnson, who confirmed that the injuries were largely superficial. In fact, the morning following the shooting, Holden was resting well and said that he hoped to be back to work in a few days. He was forty-three years old and had been with the Southern Railroad for twenty years. Fortunately, this was the first serious accident that had happened to him during that time.

Of more interest is the report in the *Journal* that, as soon as news of the shooting reached Winston, "a special train left the union station carrying Sheriff George W. Flynt, Chief of Police J.A. Thomas, Special Officer Oliver, Policemen Apple and Cofer, and Capt. Dugan to the scene of the crime for the purpose of apprehending and bringing to justice the negro who assaulted the conductor."

The paper also provided further information on Fuel Hairston, noting that Holden had known him "for a very long time, and that he was a very desperate character." Hairston's brother, too, it seems, had given the conductor trouble, and on one occasion, Holden had had to disarm him.

As word of the shooting spread, already strong feelings against Hairston began to turn to public rage. In fact, the March 24, 1912 edition of the *New York Times* reported that authorities were trying to get to Hairston before a lynch mob could. Running under the banner "Rush to Stop a Lynching," the *Times* reported:

> *A special train carrying fifteen policemen and special railroad detectives left here* [Greensboro] *to-night to aid in the capture and prevent the lynching of Fuel Hairston, a negro desperado who shot and slightly wounded a Southern Railway conductor, E.S. Holden.*
>
> *The negro is surrounded by a citizen posse. Feeling is so intense against him that trouble is feared.*

The next commentary on the rapidly evolving manhunt appeared in the *Greensboro Daily News* on Sunday, March 24. According to an account by Greensboro police chief Iseley, which was received at 2:15 a.m., Hairston had been arrested Saturday night, about midnight, at the home of his sister, some seven miles north of Summerfield, a small town in northwest Guilford County. It was also stated that the prisoner would be brought back to Greensboro before or by daylight at least. No further details were available at the time the paper went to press, although it ventured to say that "it is thought that no one of the strong posse was injured, or that there was any trouble in effecting the capture, the negro not suspecting that officers were so near."

It seems that when word reached authorities in Greensboro as to Hairston's whereabouts, a special train was quickly assembled there to transport a posse to the site. The train, consisting of a small engine and cab, together with its passengers, left Greensboro about 8:00 p.m. headed for Summerfield. The reporter characterized the officers as especially experienced. The *Daily News* account continued:

> *The posse on the special consisted of Southern railway agent E.W. Oliver, who was in charge of the train; Sheriff B.E. Jones, Police Chief Thomas of Winston-Salem; Police Chief Iseley, of Greensboro; Commissioner of Public Safety, E.A. Brown, of this city, and day officers Foushee, Bray, Hepler, Skeens and Gardner and deputized railroad men. The party was joined at Summerfield by a deputized body of officers who went with them in special conveyance to the place where the negro was thought to be hiding, which is seven miles almost due north of Summerfield, and just over the Rockingham county line. On account of a loaded wagon Commissioner Brown and Officers Bray and Gardner returned to the city last night after 12 o'clock by automobile.*

The story also gave some information on how the fugitive had been found. It seems that immediately after the shooting, Hairston left Kernersville and headed to his sister's in Rockingham County. His plan was to hide there until he could make good his escape. He informed his sister that he had come for a visit of a day or two but told her nothing of the shooting. His sister then went to the home of Robert Cummings to obtain provisions needed to entertain her brother. She told Cummings about her brother's visit. Cummings, who had read an account of the shooting in the *Daily News*, said nothing about it, but he later notified railway officials of what he had learned, and they quickly planned for Hairston's capture. As the paper put it, "The fact that his sister didn't know the grave offense he had committed, was largely responsible for his being located last night."

While reporting to authorities, Cummings was deputized over the phone and instructed to gather a group of citizens and keep the house where Hairston was hiding under surveillance until the posse could arrive.

Acting on the information provided by Cummings, the special train and posse headed off to Summerfield, the end of the rail line, where a wagon was waiting to carry the party the rest of the way to the Hairston house. After the officers arrived in Summerfield, there was no further communication from them because the telegraph and telephone lines had been shut down to ensure that Hairston did not get wind of what was afoot.

According to the *Daily News* account, "It was thought that the house would be surrounded and watched until morning," especially since "last night was very unfavorable to pursuers on account of the drizzly rain and the dark." The story continued:

> *The roads to the place where the negro was thought to be in hiding were not of the best and there was little wonder that the reports came in so slow, a drive of a total of 14 miles besides the capturing of the negro, being among the hardships of the posse.*

The account in the paper also noted:

> *Railroad men were of a warpath mood last night, and feeling was not at low ebb among them by any means. If they had laid their hands on Hairston unrestrained matters might have gone bad.*

Despite these adverse conditions, the posse left Greensboro determined to bring Hairston back before a rougher form of justice could take its course. As the paper put it, "Special Agent Oliver left here with the determination to bring his man back in some form, and the men who went with him were determined, being officers of hardiness and experience."

At least some members of the posse thought Hairston might put up a fight. One of the local police officers who had arrested Hairston on a previous occasion for a small offense said "that while he was a mean negro, he did not regard him as ferocious, although he might do something desperate should he be driven to a corner." However, he said he believed that "the officers would land the negro unless he secured some intimation of their presence and escaped in the darkness."

News that Hairston had in fact been captured reached the public on the morning of March 24, when the *Winston-Salem Journal* published an account of his arrest:

> *After surrounding him in a hut where he had taken refuge ten miles north of Summerfield in Rockingham county, a posse of officers and citizens, led by Chief of Police J.A. Thomas of this city, Special Officer E.W. Oliver, Sheriff Jones of Guilford and Chief of Police Iseley of Greensboro, this morning at 2:15 o'clock captured Fuel Hairston, the negro who shot Conductor Edward S. Holden while the conductor was boarding the train in Kernersville Friday night.*

The story of the capture had been phoned in to Greensboro and thence to the *Journal*. Still, there were few real details of what had transpired, although it appeared that the posse had surrounded the house and then took Hairston by surprise, giving him no opportunity to resist.

After Hairston was taken into custody, "he was hustled towards Summerfield, closely guarded by the officers, as feeling among the citizens was high." As the *Journal* noted:

> *The attempt to take the life of Conductor Holden, who is one of the most popular men in the employ of the Southern on the Winston-Salem division, created the intensest feelings here, as well as throughout this section. When it was learned last night that the negro had been surrounded in a hut near Summerfield by a posse of citizens vague fears of a lynching were held.*

According to the March 26 *Winston-Salem Journal*, Hairston was indeed brought to Greensboro. Later, however, he was removed to Winston-Salem in the custody of Forsyth County sheriff George W. Flynt and Special

Agent F.W. Oliver. Regarding Sheriff Flynt, the paper included the following correction:

> *By a mistake of the Greensboro informant of* The Journal, *from whom the names of the officers who led the posse that captured Hairston were obtained, it was stated Sunday morning that one of the leaders was Chief Thomas of this city, when the local chief of police was in the crowd, and the posse was led by Sheriff George W. Flynt instead. It was known at the time that Sheriff Flynt was somewhere searching for the negro and had been searching for him almost continuously, without even allowing himself time for sleep, since the assault on Conductor Holden was made.*

According to the paper, Flynt and Oliver had left Kernersville and other points on the rail line between Winston and Kernersville on Saturday afternoon. While doing so, "they got on the track of the negro and at first proceeded alone to Summerfield, where additional clues were obtained." Later, however, they returned to Greensboro, "where Sheriff Flynt manipulated the phone and found the exact location of Hairston. Over the phone he deputized a farmer of Rockingham to watch the house in which the negro was hiding until the officers could arrive."

The *Journal* concluded with the note that Hairston had been placed in the Forsyth County jail and would be given a hearing as soon as Conductor Holden was well enough to attend.

In fact, Hairston's preliminary hearing did not occur until April 7, a fact reported in another *Journal* article of that date. According to the story, the hearing took place before Colonel J.C. Bessent, a local Winston-Salem justice of the peace. It is likely that the examination took only a short while, as Hairston pleaded guilty. His bond was set at $500, which he was unable to meet, and so he was remanded to jail to await further proceedings. At the same hearing, Hairston was also charged with carrying a concealed weapon, presumably the weapon he used to shoot Conductor Holden. He pleaded guilty to this charge as well and was bound over to superior court under a bond fixed at $50.

There can be little doubt but that Hairston received considerable time in prison for shooting Conductor Holden. But his exact sentence cannot be determined, as no further accounts of the case have as yet been located.

Edward Holden, the wounded train conductor, was the son of Henry L. Holden and Mary Ladosa of Guilford County. Sometime after the incident, Edward and his wife, Gertie Zigler, moved to Greensboro. Holden died there on April 28, 1928, and was buried in Green Hill Cemetery in that city, where his mother and father and other members of the Holden family also rest. The name on his stone is given as "Edwin Seymour Holden." His wife, Gertie, died on February 8, 1960, at the age of eighty-three. She, too, was interred in Green Hill.

A LITTLE CHILD SHALL LEAD THEM

One day during the Christmas season of 1922, the citizens of Kernersville were astonished to witness one of the most amazing sights the small town had ever seen: a young lad gallantly marching the town's chief of police, arms pointed heavenward, along the main street at the point of a very large revolver. The spectacle was made all the more memorable because the police chief, Charlie Dillard, was a fellow of considerable physique, weighing at least 225 pounds.

Probably much to the lasting embarrassment of Dillard, two local papers got wind of what happened and ran expositions of the entire episode. One of these appeared in the December 30, 1922 edition of the *Winston-Salem Journal*, while a second appeared in the *Greensboro Daily News* on the same date. The former paper ran the story under the following headline:

> *Boy Marches Cop Around At Point Of Big Pistol*
> *Pulls Six-Shooter Stunt on Chief of Police in*
> *Kernersville and Demands That His Dad*
> *Be Freed From Jail.*

The Greensboro paper heralded the event with this banner:

> *KERNERSVILLE CHIEF CAPTURED BY A YOUTH*
> *Charlie Dillard, 225-Pound Officer,*
> *Marched to Jail By 13-Year-old Boy*
> *WAS SEEKING HIS DAD*

While the facts as recounted in the two stories vary slightly in terms of details, they agree on the essentials. This is how things developed.

A young boy named Manuel Hendrick (his surname is given as Kendrick in the *Greensboro Daily News* account) had

> *spent his early boyhood with his daddy in the hills of Henry County, Virginia. Beneath the shady fastnesses of the ivy-covered brooks many a mountain still trickled away, and little Hendrick's father, W.T. Hendrick, learned to sip again and again of the mountain brew that brings fond memories and golden dreams.*

However, when Manuel was thirteen, his father abandoned their bucolic home in the hills and moved the family from Henry County to the small Piedmont, North Carolina town of Kernersville. There

> *the blood of adventure ran deep in the veins of the young lad from the mountains, and the change was quite too much for his adventurous soul.*

> *However, he attended school regularly and behaved himself in the best of style. His lust for adventure was satisfied with an occasional visit to the movies in the little town in which he lived. Here he could see played out before his very eyes the daring stunts of Cowboy Bill, who, single-handed, rescued his friend from the band of mountain bandits.*

On the Friday before Christmas, Manuel went to the movie theatre in town where pictures of the Wild West were being unreeled. "There he saw men of great daring accomplishing great deeds with nothing more than a huge revolver to aid them." At that time, the theatre in Kernersville, called the Nymph, was located where 116 North Main Street is today. This theatre, or "show" as many locals called it in those days, had originally been a silent picture theatre with a piano played by a member of the Watson family who ran a grocery store in town.

As fate would have it, the same day that Manuel watched the show, his father, perhaps celebrating the Christmas spirit that doubtless pervaded the town, felt the call for a drink of the mountain brew he remembered so fondly from his Henry County days. Unfortunately, Kendrick "hooked up with a quantity of wildcat liquor" instead. As one would imagine, this near-lethal concoction "had a terrible effect—it wasn't smooth and mellow like the dew from the ivy-covered still, but it carried a knockout." One suspects, however, that whether smooth or not, the liquor's effect would have been the same, and soon Kendrick was three sheets to the wind.

About this same time, Chief Dillard happened along and placed Kendrick under arrest, "on the charge of imbibing too much of the forbidden fluid," and took him along to the town's calaboose.

Somehow Manuel learned of his father's distress. The *Journal* version says that, as the boy watched the movie, a "friend [or foe] slipped into the movie house and told him that his dad was in jail," while the Greensboro paper said that when the picture was over, he returned home, where he heard what had befallen his father. In any case, the boy procured "his dad's six-shooter, rammed it in his jeans, and set out for the rescue."

Before long, Manuel sighted Chief Dillard talking to a man on the street. The boy wasted not a moment but walked bravely up to him, tapped on his shoulder to gain his attention and announced, "Chief, I'd like to speak with you a minute." At that, the chief glanced around and, seeing only a boy, "paid no heed and resumed his conversation." Undeterred, young Manuel waited "until the friend of the chief had departed" and then repeated to the police constable that he wanted to speak with him.

According to the newspaper account, "The officer turned around, and found himself staring down the barrel of a big horse pistol in the hands of the lad." No doubt taken aback, Dillard asked, "What do you mean, boy? Put up that pistol." But young Manuel, having none of that, replied, "Nothing doing. I mean that I am going to put a hole through you if you don't let my daddy out of jail."

Seeing the determined look in the boy's eyes, and realizing that the boy was serious through and through, Chief Dillard decided not to test the young lad's patience and slowly lifted his hands.

Trying to stall the boy until he could think of a plan, the officer replied that he had left the jail keys at home. "Well just get in front of this gun and march home after them," said the boy.

Having run out of delaying tactics, the chief decided he better do as young Kendrick demanded, and "the big policeman marched down the street, secured the key, and marched back to the jail, while the astounded populace looked on with bulging eyes and growing wonder."

"On reaching the jail the boy commanded the officer to enter the jail first, and as the officer got inside he grabbed his pistol from a nearby table, and wheeled on the boy, who was taken unawares."

"Drop that gun, or I'll kill you!" ordered the officer.

Seeing that the tables had been turned, the boy "did as commanded and in turn became the prisoner."

According to the account carried in the *Journal*, Manuel was taken to Winston-Salem and tried in juvenile court. As it turned out, on the probation officer's recommendation the boy was let go under probation, "conditioned on his reporting once each week to the mayor of Kernersville to show good behavior."

As the reporter noted, "It was quite a stunt to be pulled off in a town so quiet and unpretentious as Kernersville, and the folk down there are still wondering how it all happened."

It seems that was not quite the end of the story, however, as it was reported in the next day's *Journal* that "some one with a sense of humor had inscribed over the jail door in Kernersville" the following inscription taken from Isaiah 11:6: "A Little Child Shall Lead Them."

It is suspected that Chief Dillard found little humor in this added insult. He no doubt endured many more ribbings about the boy with the gun in the days and years that followed.

THE QUEEN OF VIRGINIA BOOTLEGGERS

In the summer of 2008, the North Carolina Collection Gallery in the Wilson Library at the University of North Carolina at Chapel Hill staged an exhibit called Satan in a Bottle: A History of the Production & Control of Alcoholic Beverages in North Carolina. Writing about the exhibit in the July 21, 2008 *Raleigh News & Observer*, J. Peder Zane noted that "when it comes to booze, North Carolina's history conjures images of spirited temperance rallies, revenue agents smashing mountain stills, and politicians and preachers condemning the 'drink demon.'" But, as Zane points out, "that history of an ever-dry state is all wet." In fact, in the early days of the state's history, "Tar Heels were known as a rough-and-tumble people who kept their friends close and their bottles closer."

However, beginning about 1825, the temperance movement, which aimed to reduce alcohol consumption throughout society, began to stir in the United States. By 1870, the movement had gained considerable strength, and its aims were expanded to include a total ban on the selling of all alcoholic drinks, including beer and wine.

Because of the political difficulties associated with such an effort, other tactics were tried. One of these involved the so-called "local option" approach, which, in simple terms, left the decision up to local communities. In North Carolina, the general assembly enacted a law in 1874 called "An Act to Prohibit the Sale of Spirituous Liquors in Townships Where the People So Determine." In effect, it allowed local elections each year, upon the petition of one-fourth of the qualified voters of any township, to "ascertain whether or not spirituous liquors shall or may be sold in said township or townships." Many communities used this law to muster support for prohibition, but not all. In 1881, a statewide vote to ban alcohol in North Carolina failed to gain enough support to pass. In fact, it was 1908 before the state finally adopted a statewide prohibition.

Evidently, Kernersville had its share of citizens who enjoyed a drink of the hard stuff now and then and even a barroom or two that catered to them. There was, of course, plenty of blockade whiskey to be had from local sources just about any time, day or night.

In Kernersville, as elsewhere, there was concern about the effects of booze on the morals of the citizenry, a subject mentioned in a piece of nicely written sarcasm that appeared in the May 31, 1883 edition of the *People's Press* of Winston:

> *The County Commissioners have granted Mr. Carter, living near the depot, right in the edge of our incorporation, license to sell liquor from three gallons up, and it is said the first week after he opened he sold to the amount of ninety dollars, and no doubt it will greatly improve the morals of our people, judging from some of the indications already apparent, and we ought to be very thankful to the Commissioners for their favor.*

The author was the Kernersville correspondent for the newspaper, the Reverend C.L. Rights, who was also the minister of Kernersville Moravian Church. Like many other religious leaders in those days, Rights was keenly interested in banning the consumption of that devil alcohol.

The good reverend returned to this topic once again in a "Kernersville Letter" that appeared in the March 13, 1884 *People's Press*:

> *Well, our friend "Ben Bounce" gave Kernersville a pretty fair showing, but he did not tell it all; he entirely left out one of the principal industries of our thriving place, Messrs. Carter & Nelson's "Drinking Saloon." It is said it proves to be a mint of money to the proprietors; they are very respectable men, and from the endorsement it has, you can't say a word against it. Of the parties that licensed it, three are leading members in the Methodist church, and one is a preacher in another church, and there is only one sinner among them; in fact, the whole thing is enveloped in an odor of sanctity, and we outsiders must bow in humble submission to the behest. Mr. Bounce congratulates us on our morals, and no doubt this is a means of increasing it; and if any persons at a distance contemplate sending their sons to the Kernersville High School, it may be an additional incentive to know that they can get a drink of beer, wine, whisky or brandy, any time day or night.*

The Nelson mentioned by Rights was probably R. Shepherd "Shep" Nelson, the same man referred to in a January 19, 1888 item in the *News and Farm* of Kernersville: "Mr. R.S. Nelson who has been running a bar-room in Winston, for the last six months, has returned to Kernersville and

opened a grocery store at his old stand. He says the tax was too high on him in Winston."

It appears that in 1888, prohibitionists in Kernersville were still hoping to eliminate the sale of liquor by adopting a local option approach, but their effort that year failed again. The information comes once more from a letter written by Reverend Rights that appeared in the June 10, 1888 *People's Press*:

> *Messrs. Editors.—Our Local Option election came off yesterday and defeated by nine votes, and that was because some weak-kneed Christians*

> *did not vote at all. Rev. Sandy Ring came down with his cohorts "as wolves in the fold," and every nerve was strained to the utmost on the part of the license party; but while they beat us, they did not seem to be very jubilant over their success. Five years ago they beat us five to one, and this time they got it, but it was like the Dutchman's getting to heaven, "by a mighty tight squeeze."*
>
> *I must say a good word for the respectable part of the colored people,—they rallied for local option to a man, and if some white people would have done their duty, we would have it today. Well, some folks will have the chance to drink mean whiskey another year, and perhaps it will kill them off, and we will get local option for all after that.*
>
> *The vote stood Local Option, 101*
> *License, 110*

Incidentally, the Reverend Sanford Ring was a Primitive Baptist preacher serving in the Kernersville area at the time.

As stated earlier, statewide prohibition was adopted in North Carolina in 1908. However, efforts to ban the manufacture and sale of liquor on a nationwide basis continued unabated. Finally, Congress drafted the Eighteenth Amendment to the United States Constitution, which brought total Prohibition to the nation on January 29, 1920. It remained in effect until 1933, when it was rescinded in its entirety by the Twenty-first Amendment.

Not surprisingly, the legislation did little if anything to quell the continuing demand for alcoholic products. Since legal enterprises could no longer meet the demand, illegal ones stepped in, and the bootleg profession boomed. Zane, in his article discussing the "Satan in a Bottle Exhibit," noted that "such strict statutes became the best friend of moonshiners. They built secret stills and fast cars—helping lay the foundation for NASCAR racing—to elude the authorities and satisfy a thirsty public." As an illustration, in 1921, 95,933 illicit distilleries, stills, still works and fermentors were seized by authorities. That number grew to 172,537 in 1925 and to 282,122 in 1930.

North Carolina probably had more than its fair share of bootleggers, and some of them included Kernersville in their areas of operation. An especially interesting case in point involved a so-called rumrunner from Virginia. Of special note is that this particular "he" was in fact a she dressed in male attire.

The first account of her arrest appeared on December 22, 1930, in the *Burlington Daily Times*. According to the reporter, "Nattily togged out in male attire—suit, hat and topcoat—a woman who Chief George Fontaine of

Kernersville said was 'the cream of Virginia's bootleggers,' came to grief in that village last night." Fontaine, it was reported, "found two five-gallon cans of corn whiskey and five one-gallon cans of apple brandy in her automobile." It appears that when this lady was apprehended, "she pulled ten $20 bills from her pocket, thrust them at him and asked to be let go." Fontaine, however, refused the attempted bribe and instead brought her to Winston-Salem, where she was charged with violating Prohibition laws. She was held in jail overnight and then released the following day "on a $500 bond furnished by a Winston-Salem Man," on the condition that she appear before the mayor of Kernersville for a hearing. Chief Fontaine "said the woman always traveled alone, dressed as a man, and had been running liquor four years to his own knowledge."

The *Winston-Salem Journal* also ran this story on December 23, 1930. In this version, the woman was identified as "Gene Tatum, 26, of Patrick County, Virginia." Tatum was said to be the "queen of Virginia bootleggers." Fontaine claimed that the woman "was en route to High Point with the liquor and had been distributing whiskey in this section for some time."

The *Greensboro Daily News* also found this story too tantalizing to omit and ran it in its Christmas Eve edition:

> *Tatum, whose appellation "Queen of Virginia Bootleggers" has made her an aspirant for the American hall of fame or infamy according to individual viewpoints, was a "guest" in the county jail last night after being lodged there by federal officers who brought her to this city from Kernersville. She is being held in default of $1000 bond for appearance in federal court having waived preliminary hearing Tuesday.*
>
> *The Queen was arrested Sunday night in Kernersville by Chief of Police George Fontaine of that place who is credited with the statement that the woman has been plying her trade as a bootlegger for four years or more with immunity from the law. At the time of the arrest she was attired in men's garb and driving a Hudson coach loaded with 10 gallons of whisky and five gallons of brandy, officers reported.*

Elsewhere in the *Daily News* story, it was reported that a federal warrant had been sworn out against Tatum and that deputy U.S. marshal V.C. Bradley and J.L. Osteen, acting deputy Prohibition administrator, had brought the defendant to Greensboro. She was charged with possession and transportation of illegal liquor. According to the two officers, "Gene told them that she wears men's clothing all the time and the officers admitted last night that she would pass for a male." They "described her as a comely young woman of marked masculine features." While she was being brought from Kernersville to Greensboro, Tatum told the officers that she had attended business school in the latter city several years ago.

George Fontaine, the officer who first arrested Tatum, was himself quite a striking figure in the Kernersville area for many years. He was a big man, probably close to six and a half feet tall, usually seen in earlier days wearing a pistol and blackjack strapped to his belt and riding a motorcycle. He was at one time a member of the North Carolina Highway Patrol. From 1935 until his death in January 1963, he was a deputy sheriff in Forsyth County, North Carolina.

BIBLIOGRAPHY

Books

Appleton's Annual Cyclopaedia and Register of Important Events of the Year 1896. New York: D. Appleton and Company, 1897.

Bondeson, Jan. *Buried Alive: The Terrifying History of Our Most Primal Fear*. New York: W.W. Norton & Company, 2001.

Bower, Jennifer Bean. *Winston & Salem: Tales of Murder, Mystery and Mayhem*. Charleston, SC: The History Press, 2007.

Branson's North Carolina Business Directory. Raleigh, NC: Branson & Farrar, 1866–67; 1867–68; 1869; 1872; 1877–78; 1884; 1890; and 1896.

Davies, Rodney. *The Lazarus Syndrome: Buried Alive and Other Horrors of the Undead*. New York: Barnes and Noble Books, 1998.

Emerson, Charles. *Chas. Emerson's Tobacco Belt Directory*. Greensboro, NC: Emerson, 1886.

Guide Book of N.W. North Carolina. Salem, NC: L.V. & E.T. Blum, Printers, 1878.

Henderson, Archibald. *North Carolina: The Old North State and the New*. Chicago: Lewis Publishing Company, 1941.

Körner, Jules Gilmer, Jr. *Joseph of Kernersville*. Durham, NC: Seeman Printery, Inc., 1958.

Post, Melville Davisson. *The Man Hunters*. Whitefish, MT: Kessinger Publishing Company, 2005.

Post Offices and Postmasters of North Carolina: Colonial to USPS. N.p.: North Carolina Postal History Society, 1996.

Robbins, Dr. D.P. *Descriptive Sketch of Winston-Salem*. Winston, NC: Sentinel Job Print, 1888.

Stanley, Donald W. *Forsyth County Cemetery Records*. Winston-Salem, NC: Hunter Publishing Company, 1977.

Newspapers

Anaconda Standard, Anaconda, Montana
Bee, Danville, Virginia
Boston Globe, Boston, Massachusetts
Burlington Daily Times, Burlington, North Carolina
Cedar Falls Gazette, Cedar Falls, Iowa
Charlotte Observer, Charlotte, North Carolina
Daily Huronite, Sioux Falls, South Dakota
Daily Workman, Greensboro, North Carolina
Greensboro Daily News, Greensboro, North Carolina
Greensboro North State, Greensboro, North Carolina
Greensboro Patriot, Greensboro, North Carolina
Greensboro Telegram, Greensboro, North Carolina
High Point Enterprise, High Point, North Carolina
Kernersville News, Kernersville, North Carolina
Kingston Daily Freeman. Kingston, New York
Landmark, Statesville, North Carolina
Morning News, Greensboro, North Carolina
News and Farm, Kernersville, North Carolina
News & Observer, Raleigh, North Carolina
New York Times, New York, New York
New York Tribune, New York, New York
People's News, Kernersville, North Carolina
People's Press, Salem, North Carolina
Portsmouth Daily Times, Portsmouth, Ohio
Robesonian, Lumberton, North Carolina
Silver Advocate, Kernersville, North Carolina
Times, Richmond, Virginia
Union Republican, Winston-Salem, North Carolina
Virginia Pilot & Norfolk Landmark, Portsmouth, Virginia
Washington Bee, Washington, D.C.
Washington Post, Washington, D.C.

Western Sentinel, Winston-Salem, North Carolina
Winston-Salem Journal, Winston-Salem, North Carolina

Periodicals

American Illustrated Magazine no. 1 (September 1905–June 1906).
Burial Reformer no. 1 (April 1905–December 1908).
Forsyth County Genealogical Society Journal no. 1 (Fall 1982–present).